Overcoming Adversity in Entrepreneurship

We Did It, and So Can You!

Andrew Izumi and Gina Taylor

And 26 Other Leading Entrepreneurs

ISBN: 978-1-64184-236-5 (paperback)
ISBN: 978-1-64184-237-2 (ebook)

DEDICATION

This book is dedicated to two special groups of people: the aspiring entrepreneur and the successful entrepreneur.

To the aspiring entrepreneur. Have you ever wondered if there was something more to life than your 9–5 job? Have you ever been inspired to really live out your dream and make a positive impact in this world? We are all here to tell you that it is possible! There will be adversities that you face along the way, but do not give up on your dream. Take a leap of faith. All of us have struggled at some point, but that did not stop us from accomplishing what we have set foot on this earth to do.

To the successful entrepreneur. We feel your pain and want to connect with you. Life has not been roses and cookies all day, every day, but we all have gone through hardships together and succeeded against all odds. You inspire us to live lives that are fulfilling, and we respect the risks that you have taken as well. Keep crushing it in your business, and enjoy the stories to follow. We look forward to connecting with you in the future.

FOREWORD
BY JAMES SMILEY

Entrepreneurship is 80% hardship, which doesn't fit the fantasy that most people have. People don't really want to know about the hardship. That doesn't mean that somebody who's saying, "Hey, I went from pizza boy to millionaire" didn't actually do that, but there's a lot more to the story than that. If you hear someone on a webinar say, "In 10 minutes, I'm going to teach you how to make $17,000 a day with a web funnel," don't be naive enough to think that you will definitely make $17,000 a day.

I actually tried this once because I was optimistic enough to think it might work. I tried it; It didn't work. I didn't make $17,000, but I found out how to make money. There is a fine balance between not being unrealistically optimistic and being too pessimistic not to try anything.

For me, my whole entrepreneurship journey has been about overcoming adversity. I really believe that everybody who wants to be an entrepreneur has to experience fairly similar adversities. We definitely all have the same amount of time in the day. No one has a 40-hour day; everyone only has 24. So, time is not an excuse. And that's one of the biggest excuses. That's only one excuse, but there are other adversities and challenges.

There are excuses that people get away with, but one thing you have to realize is that there's this victim mentality that's become really big now. And it's really crept into entrepreneurism. I've seen the evolution and change in people's attitudes. It's staggering how much, in the last two years, the victimhood mentality has come into a lot of people. And it's not that they're bad people, that they're not called to do what they're supposed to do, or that their vision isn't real. It's just that the victimhood mentality holds them back. And the biggest thing with that is the number of people who become victims. When things get tough, they have to push the blame somewhere else because it just can't be them.

They're like, "Well, I did this, but your system didn't work." But that's like saying, in sports, if the coach calls a play a certain way, and you're the running back, and you get the ball, if there are a bunch of people over there, the good running backs run the other way. It doesn't matter which way the play was called; they're smart enough to make a decision and own the moment. That's why only 2% to 5% of entrepreneurs are actually going to make it to the big time. They get there by taking ownership of everything.

I made my first six figures when I was in my 20s when I was part of a software company that IPO'd. I learned a lot from a lot of smart people when I was quite young. It wasn't magic, and I wasn't smarter than everybody. I learned to leverage other people's ideas, thoughts, knowledge base, and experience so I didn't have to go through all of those struggles myself. But somebody told me, "James, there are only two types of businesses. There's the drama business, and there's your business. You don't have enough time, energy, motivation, and resources to be involved in both."

If you take that advice to heart, it will change your entire life. It will change your revenue and change the way your clients see you. If you're the type of person who gets into courses and coaching programs and you're always talking about people behind their back, you're in the drama business. And that is why your business isn't working. You don't ever hear multi-millionaires like Russell Brunson or Tony Robbins say that's how they got big. I challenge you not to get hung up by that.

A big thing for me is the art of leverage, and I'm really big into partnerships. Like all major entrepreneurs—Tony Robbins, Tai Lopez, Russell Brunson, anybody—they all have great partners. And they have multiple partners and multiple businesses. The reason why most people never succeed in partnerships is that they can't deal with bad partners. But that's a part of what comes with partnerships; eventually, you're going to have a bad partner.

I once went to give a mastermind event in Austin, Texas, with one of my business partners. It was him and me in our coaching program. On the day of the event, he called me up and said that he couldn't make the event because his wife was sick. He asked me to pray for his wife. It was sad, and we had a moment of silence in our business mastermind for his wife. That's how serious we were about this. Well, lo and behold, I found out he was actually in the same town. He traveled to the same town and went to a different event! Here I was, staying up all night to prepare till 5:30 in the morning, slept 30 minutes, did his teaching for 13 hours, and went the next day to talk for 8 hours. And here was my partner down the street wanting to revenue share the company.

I didn't let that moment become a big thing where I started gossiping about him. I'll be honest, I screwed it up for a day because I was pretty pissed when it first happened. But I calmed myself enough to think, *You know, I can't let this determine what people think of me forever and also to the dream clients that I have out there. If I go out there and bash this guy, which I have every right to, the people I respect are not going to think very highly of that.* That's a huge part of overcoming a challenge that's in a partnership, a deal, or with a client. You have to choose to take the high ground.

If you really dig into my life, you'll find I lost my son in 2015. It was a tragic thing. He was born with a medical condition, a terminal illness. When I lost him, it was devastating. I mean, it was *devastating!* I cried every day for a year, it was that hard. But I chose to try to find out the purpose. I asked myself, *Why did God allow this to happen to me? Why am I involved in this?*

At this moment, you need to have that vision and have that purpose and passion for going on and doing something greater. I felt that something divine happened in my life. It became life-changing for the better.

Whether it's an entrepreneur, someone in the corporate world, or even in their personal life, a lot of people don't take ownership these days. They place the blame on somebody else, or there's an excuse, or there's a reason why something didn't get done. "Well, you know, I had this happen, or he said that, she said this." In the end, none of those things really matter because the ball doesn't move forward at all.

Even if it actually could have been someone else's fault, it literally doesn't matter. You know, the business gods are not going to come and IPO your company because you got screwed. That's where true entrepreneurs become defined.

Any Joe Schmo can go out and create an LLC, or create brands, or get a business card, or change their name on their Facebook page, or get a free client. I am saying an entrepreneur, by definition, is someone who is willing to take risk—specifically, financial risk. You have to be willing to put yourself out there, and if you're not willing to do it, or if you want to blame somebody else for causing this or that thing to happen to you, then entrepreneurship might not be your game. So step up your game, overcome adversity in entrepreneurship, and WIN BIG! Congratulations to everyone who is reading this book because you will find inspiring stories of triumph over adversity to motivate and inspire you.

CONTENTS

IT'S ALL IN THE FAMILY

by Gina Taylor

As long as I can remember, I have always been what typically would be labeled a loner. To me, I just didn't want to be like everyone else. I had a burning desire to be a free-spirited, journey-seeking, nature-loving cowgirl. Growing up in the 70s, I certainly didn't fit the mold for society's expectations. After all, Girl Scouts wore skirts, and what kind of cowgirl would do that? While the Girl Scout crowd hung out at recess at the monkey bars and hopscotch, this little cowgirl was happily in the saddle of the recycled tractor tire partially submerged in the dirt, and I was blazing trails through my imaginary countryside.

I was blessed to grow up in a family whose legacy was founded on entrepreneurism. My grandfathers were exceptional pioneers and laid a great foundation for my parents, aunts, uncles, cousins—and me. My paternal grandfather raised cattle (which is where the cowgirl genetics came from), and my maternal grandfather's knack for growing superior produce would soon become a roadside produce stand and the best place to play hide and seek for my cousins and myself. The roadside produce stand would eventually become a well-known grocery store in South Park, a smaller town on the outskirts of Seattle.

Now, this wasn't just your typical grocery store; it was the heartbeat of my family, my first real paycheck, and my first lessons on the dynamics of running a profitable business with your entire family. If that isn't a challenge, I don't know what is. To add one more dynamic, the whole family is Italian, so we were dealing with passionate, expressive people, and "Mumma Mia's" were rolling off the tongue, and hands of expression were going every which way while shoppers were shopping, deliveries were being received, and the lunch crowd was swarming in for fried chicken and potato wedges.

This may all sound like a bunch of craziness (and yes, it was) but the life lessons from being in this unique work setting were second to none. What other job can you have that you are with your entire family on a daily basis? The lessons were many, and I'm grateful for all of them, but I have to say that the lessons I learned from my grandfather were priceless and deeply embedded in me.

My grandfather made sure that everybody worked hard, customers were assisted, and the produce looked just right. He was a master of customer service and was always present to what was happening around him. His attention to quality and presentation of the appearance within the store was amazing. The love he gave that business was amazing, and it flowed into everyone who worked there. Our work culture was unique, my grandmother and aunts handled the bookkeeping and cashiering, and all the other departments were handled by cousins. My uncles tailored a fresh meat market, and I was the deli queen.

Our family's grocery store became quite the landmark and eventually was sold due to the big box store competition. For some family members, this became their retirement. For myself and my cousins, it became our first taste of following our own passions and establishing businesses of our own.

This was my first chance to reel in all of those fantasies of riding horses all day. I believe, in some crazy way, that my passion for horses was genetically part of my being, but over the first fifteen years of my life was fueled by no other than my grandfather, my mother, and a special horse named Seattle Slew. Although this horse was the kind who ran on a race track, the buzz he created in our town was nothing less than catchable. The second and confirming influence came when I was fortunate enough to take a vacation to the Great Teton Valley in Wyoming. This was what sealed the deal. The day I sat on the back of a horse and rode off onto the mountainside was the day that I knew that was what I was put on this planet to do.

The peaceful tranquility of looking across the valley at that beautiful Teton mountain range, and being on a horse at the same time, was nothing shy of heaven on earth. I sat around the campfire that night thinking to myself, *Wow, that was amazing, and we paid fifty dollars each for that one-hour loop into the hillside and back.* (This was the early 80s, so fifty dollars was worth a lot more money at the time.) The wheels and the entrepreneurial bug became embedded in my heart.

The only dilemma at this point was that I lived in a harbor town with beautiful views of the Olympic Mountains and majestic Mount Rainier, but giving guided horse tours around town just wasn't the experience I was looking to deliver. Also, I had just become Miss Burien Seafair, which where I grew up is a huge honor and an exceptional opportunity.

I began my journey as a princess in the Seafair Court. This was my introduction to cultural events, public speaking, entertainment production, dance choreography, community service, and learning how to walk at an angle downstairs in a swimsuit and high heels with confidence and grace. It was a lot of work! It was twelve weeks of personal appearances, dress rehearsals, two parades a day, performing, signing autographs, photo-shoot sessions, and modeling at fashion shows. But it was also a time of healing and connection. I had just lost my mother to cancer the week after I had won my crown. Now, I was in a home with no mother, a father trying to hold himself together, a younger brother just entering middle school, and other family indirectly holding me up to take over where my mother had left off and keeping everyone accountable.

When I look back now, I can see I was gifted with so much more than just that experience. I had been divinely placed right where I was supposed to be at that place in my life. I was surrounded by love, encouragement, like-minded people, exceptional professionals, and a support system that became the foundation of how I approach life and how to overcome adversity in life. It wasn't pretty on the family side, and I didn't place in the pageant, but I did win Miss Congeniality. That was validation that my heart and character were still intact and that all of the adversity were actually lessons I would use in the future.

Fast forward five years, and I was now a mother, a wife, then a single parent. I had to support a family, and thus began the new grind of a 9-to-5 job. I was fortunate enough to obtain full-time employment with great benefits and room for growth. This became yet another lesson in business and how the CEO creates an A-team culture for the company. The owner was amazing. He was able to cultivate a work culture that, in today's world, most would line up and beg for a job in a company with that culture. He would make deliveries with the delivery crew, do inventory on inventory count days, and randomly show up and take the warehouse employee's out to lunch. He even took that whole part of the company on an annual five-day trip somewhere in the U.S. I cannot say enough great things about him. He was an awesome mentor on how to treat your employees. He actually cared enough that one of our conversations led to me sharing my dream of riding horses all day. He told me to follow my heart and reach for my dream.

I took his advice, and I began to plan all I would need. Starting with horses led to needing somewhere to keep horses, and the list of needs grew. Randomly reading the classified ads one day, I saw an ad for a property in Montana. I called the number and spoke with the owner, and two days later, I was in Montana looking at the property, beaming with excitement. I drove nine hours one way, to find out that, yes, it was forty acres, but it was all trees. Not a good horse property. The area was nice, and the town's services were the perfect setting to have visitors, so with a little creative searching, I eventually moved there with the intent to open a trail ride business. I knew I wanted to offer that experience, but I didn't know how or what the dynamics of running that kind of business were. I needed a mentor and had no clue where to start.

My dream sat by the wayside for what would turn into almost sixteen years. I had many life experiences in that time, some devastating and others great, but I held onto my dream and the desire to see it happen. I knew I would need horses that were exceptionally trained. I knew I needed to develop exceptional horsemanship skills to care for the horses and assure myself the guests would be safe. I also had to incorporate the fact that the world had changed so much over those sixteen years that I not only had to learn a brick-and-mortar version of business, but also a cyber version.

I have been fortunate to have had the life I have—the good, the bad, and the ugly. Every experience became a lesson and inspiration and forced me to create boundaries in some cases. Life stages are what create transformation in our lives. We should always strive to give our all and be open to learning and growing in all areas of our lives.

I knew I needed mentors in all of those areas, and I am a big advocate for the shortest path to the goal. I have been being mentored by two of the greatest horsemen to grace this earth, and I now have horsemanship skills I never knew I was capable of. I have also hired business coaches for the skills I need to survive in an online marketplace. I am now creating the foundation of an asset, not just a business. I also have a speaking coach to work with me on cultivating the perfect delivery of sharing my business with others. I sought out training as a life coach to aid in my people skills and allow me to develop an experience that will impact the lives of my customers and those who may come into my life.

I have had to do all of these things all while trying not to be known as the fitness chick. In my everyday life, fitness and motherhood have been my lifestyle. For thirty years, I have been an exceptional athlete, and fitness has dominated my life. I love it, and part of my mother's passing fueled that, but it has never been my dream. Through the skills I have obtained from coaches and mentors, I have figured out how to combine my passion for horses with my skills in fitness and nutrition and have created an epic self-empowerment fitness bootcamp. I have designed a series of lessons and activities in conjunction with horse activities, and by the end of bootcamp, my guests walk away with a personally crafted blueprint to achieve their wellness and life goals.

Our time here on this planet is precious. If you have dreams that you think about every day, don't walk toward them—run. Whether you are on a journey as an entrepreneur or considering one, set yourself up for success from the beginning. Find the mentors, hire the coaches, arm yourself with exceptional friends and acquaintances. You become the average of the people you surround yourself with. Never stop growing, and never give up on your dreams.

ABOUT GINA TAYLOR

As a leading fitness and nutrition coach, elite athlete, and mother to six beautiful children, and an exceptional passion for people and horses, Gina's over forty years of experience in these industries has rewarded her with great joy to witness the transformation and results her clients have achieved from the education and training she teaches.

The loss of her mother to cancer fueled her passion for educating people on the importance of knowing what's in food, how that food operates on the cellular level after being consumed, and what that means to you as a consumer. The love her mother and her shared for horses led her to bridge those two passions. Blending the healing power of horses with self-empowerment strategies and packaging led to the ultimate wellness success path creating an epic experience for her clients.

It is her passion to share, educate, and impact people of all backgrounds through knowledge and simple formulas that allow you to achieve and maintain a healthy, happy, and wealthy lifestyle. She has learned as a busy mother, wife, and entrepreneur to maintain her ideal physical self painlessly by knowing how to eat and coaching others to have the same results.

PHYSICAL PAIN—EMOTIONAL PAIN—FAILURE IS NOT AN OPTION!

by Andrew Izumi

*"You have to see failure as the beginning and the middle,
but never entertain it as the end."*

—Jessica Herrin

The following is my real-life story never shared before in public. Learn from my years of mistakes and hundreds of thousands of dollars spent on education. Navigate around the potholes and landmines and make your way to extreme clarity and profit in your business.

Driving in my car. Frost on the windows. Red lights in front and white in back. I remember the night before clearly, but this day, January 10, 2013, changed my life forever.

It was the day before my girlfriend's birthday, and we had a fantastic dinner with the family. Mabo tofu with rice and green beans. That home-cooked food was what we loved to eat. As the night wound down, I kissed her goodnight, excited about her birthday the next day. Her present was wrapped, and I was going to take her out to a nice surprise dinner. I went to sleep early, knowing I had to wake up early for work and make it home in time for the festivities.

And then—I woke up in the hospital. Where am I? Am I still asleep and dreaming? This must be a mistake! IV tubes were in my arms, bandages were around my head, and my leg was very stiff. What happened?

For the past few days, I had been in and out of consciousness, drugged up with pain meds like there was no tomorrow, and had gone through two massive surgeries. My skull was cracked, and I now had a titanium plate covering the hole. My leg femur was shattered to bits, and I had a huge titanium rod in my leg. I'm all about precious metal, but honestly, I could go for my body being back to normal.

That day, driving to work in the early morning, I was crossing the Grapevine on I-5 going north into Bakersfield, CA. My car had spun out on black ice, and I was catapulted across the highway. I'll spare you the details, but what I can tell you is I scared my family, friends, and co-workers way more than myself. I was unconscious and drugged up with the potent pain meds, and I have no memory of those three days.

After twelve months of physical rehab, three days a week, and two and a half hours per session, I was back to ninety percent. There was no way this car accident was going to keep me from moving forward. I went back to my nine-to-five job, but there was something missing. I was making good money, it was easy, but what was missing? I had just gone through this traumatic accident and was feeling a bit dissatisfied with life.

I applied and was accepted as a sales manager at a Fortune 500 company. Surely, this would be my last career move. Having a top job at a Fortune 500 company and making well over six figures—this was the dream. I did my job well and sold, sold, sold, sold, and sold again. I was having fun, traveling, meeting new people, and solving problems day in and day out. The company provided me with a cell phone, laptop, car, and expense report. Free hotels, sushi dinners, prestige—and fine whiskey at company events. Most days, I was hardly paying any bills. Sitting on top of the sales leader chart, I was awarded the Rain Maker program, sending a few other select sales managers and me across the globe to an all-expenses-paid trip to Florida. But then it happened again. What was next? Where was my promotion? How do I keep learning?

Have you ever been sitting at your nine-to-five job, and had to listen to your manager tell you that you need to wait for someone to retire in order to take their job? Or maybe, you are the one who is listening to promotion promise after promotion promise that never seem to come true. If I am speaking to you, know that you can change that. I quit and took another job! It felt good to write that letter of resignation, even though deep down I was scared to leave and venture into the unknown. I had just accepted a job with a large competitor and was ready to get started immediately.

Just as this happened, the previous vice-president of sales called me into a meeting. He discussed my options for promotion and gave me a timeline of when I would get my promotion. (I hope you know where I am going with this.) The promise was six months, and I was jumping for joy. Wow, the company really was trying to keep me and did value my service. After being a loyal employee for four years, I felt it was only right that I allowed my company to go out of their way and try to accommodate. Feeling really bad about resigning my acceptance to the competitor, I was still excited about the opportunity that was in front of me. I mean, if the vice-president of sales says it's going to happen, then surely it will come true.

But as you can imagine, six months went by, then eight, then twelve. I had to have a conversation about this. Times had changed, and the promotion position was no longer on the table. I do understand that priorities change for companies, but unfortunately, I could not wait for things to get better. Taking the reins, I applied to another company to get my promotion. I was accepted, and I gladly said my goodbyes and moved on.

This is where it gets juicy. Have I had enough of a struggle yet? Not yet. Although my new company promised to allow me to take the driver seat and run my region as I pleased, this was not the case. I wasn't going to wait another five years to figure out what I had already been through, so off I went again. This time into entrepreneurship.

The story is not over, but I want you to take something extremely critical from this chapter so far. Hardships and failures are no excuse for halting your progress. Do not allow other people, things, or circumstances get in the way of you accomplishing your goals and dreams. You may have heard the proverb, "Fool me once, shame on you; fool me twice, shame on me." We all go through life with hardships and undesirable circumstances, but the best of us learn from each experience and push forward. We don't make the same mistake more than once, and each failure is only a positive learning experience for us to use in the future. They make you wiser and less prone to future errors.

If you are reading this book, I know you are thinking or have thought the same thing I am about to mention. I have had many conversations with friends and family. Is it better to invest in others, or is it better to invest in yourself? I am not saying that playing the stock market or taking on joint ventures is not a good idea investing in others, but if you are reading this book and want to find out what happens next, I urge you to believe and invest in yourself.

I'm not going to try and fool you here. Entrepreneurship is tricky, competitive, and even overwhelming at times. But toward the end of this chapter, I reveal how to simplify the process and get results quickly. There is a true secret here for all the experts out there, but it is critical that you understand the rest of my journey before we get to the gold.

I sat on the floor of my living room with my computer open, credit card in hand, ready to make the best decision of my life. Not! I had been swindled by an Internet scam. "Invest $15,000 with us, and we'll show you the way to run your successful business over the Internet and make hundreds of thousands online within months." Unfortunately, this was not the case. I had learned how to run an email campaign and set up my website, but where was the business part? That company was not invested in my success.

As I continued my journey, never giving up, I ran into not one, two, or three, but four other services that promised to do something that was never achieved. Looking at this in a positive light, I was able to learn something different each time. I was now in the hole $23,500, but I was much wiser than before. What an awesome experience I had gone through. In less than a year, I had learned so many valuable lessons worth way more than what I had spent. The key is to fail fast and learn quickly from your mistakes instead of waiting for answers to come to you. This waiting can take a very long time, and very possibly, the answers will never come.

This book is about overcoming adversity and not dwelling on past negative experiences. Every successful entrepreneur has a positive mental attitude (PMA) and takes every loss as a lesson. Pete, my third-grade baseball coach, taught me PMA, and it has stuck with me ever since. This is why I now want to share with you some key points that I have learned from these experiences.

The lessons I am about to share with you are only if you consider yourself knowledgeable in a certain category, are an action taker and willing to push the ball forward, are willing to strive for a better more fulfilling life, and most of all, you want to impact others around you positively. I want you to take this advice as not only something that will save you thousands of dollars in education but also as information that you will use for the greater good of others.

Remember how I said before that if you believe in yourself that you should invest in yourself? Well, here is the secret sauce. You are brilliant and are considered to be an expert in your field of choice. You have the ability to help others and make a positive impact on other's lives. You do not need some type of fancy certification, college graduate degree, Ph.D., or other for this. All that is necessary is the know-how and will to help others succeed. Whether you are a software developer, rock climber, knitting artist, martial arts instructor, yoga enthusiast, foreign language expert, or marketing mastermind, you have the tools you need to serve others are your highest level.

Out in the marketplace, there are a lot of "get rich quick" opportunities. Maybe it's software that you should develop or an ecommerce store you should set up. Maybe it's an online funnel-building opportunity that will get you to six or even seven figures of income. These are all great opportunities, but what I can tell you is you need to go with what you are already an expert in, and even more importantly, what is already your passion. Do not let others sway you into following their path when you can follow your own.

Let me use myself as an example. At the beginning of my career, I thought that software was my golden ticket to millions of dollars. Wrong! Software is superb, and I can't say enough great things about it. But for me, this was not the correct direction to move in. My background and my passion were in selling high-ticket or high-value products. I mean, I even went off the path from my college degree in engineering management from The George Washington University to be a sales manager right out of college. What kind of engineer graduates after spending $213,740 on his college degree to become a sales manager? All I can tell you is that I loved it, and it came naturally to me. As you can tell from the beginning of this chapter, I was always driven by sales and wanted that promotion. I always was driven by wanting more in my career.

After over ten years in sales, always being at the top of my competitors and colleagues, what was I doing trying to create software? Was I crazy? As you start out on your own entrepreneurial journey, the key to success is to go with what you already know and like. Don't be tempted to go down someone else's path. Trust me; it leads nowhere, and you will not be happy with the result.

This is why I created my program, High Ticket Momentum, where I teach other coaches, consultants, and entrepreneurs how to create and sell more high-ticket products over $2,000. If you have the knowledge and can teach others how to improve a specific part of their life, you are an expert. Yes, an expert. In this program, you learn how to command a high-ticket price, make your customers feel understood, deliver your high-ticket product, and more. Learn to sell more products, command higher prices, and enjoy more of your life that you have been missing. The sale is what makes this all happen. I am excited to share my knowledge gained from selling over $100 million worth of products, working with two Fortune 10 companies, and commanding prices up to $218,000. You can check out my free training at highticketmomentum.com.

So, does this make sense? Does this message resonate with you? The world is full of opportunities, but choosing the correct option is essential. Make sure it is something that gives you the energy to get up in the morning and gives you the drive to ensure that your customers and clients succeed. This is the key.

In any business, there are three essential moving parts.

- Yourself (the Expert)
- Your customer (the Client)
- Your distributor (the Marketer)

All three pieces of this puzzle are essential to a successful working relationship. The Expert needs to be able to deliver the service. The Client needs to have a positive transformational change. The Marketer needs to get the service in front of the right client. All three of these moving parts need to mutually benefit for a long-term, successful business to operate. I call it the win/win/win.

My main goal for you is for you to learn from my failures and apply these lessons to your life. I have three simple secrets:

Secret #1. Adversity and failure will come. Always swing the bat and learn from every experience you have, pushing yourself to improve.

Secret #2. Follow your passion and live each moment of your life doing what you were meant to do.

Secret #3. Make a profitable career out of your expert skill. The more you can serve and benefit your customer, the more you can charge for your product. (Learn more about my eight-week method at highticketmomentum.com)

As we wrap up this chapter, I want to ensure you take away as much value as possible. One of the keys to success is taking massive action quickly and learning from every experience even quicker. The reason Gina and I put this book together is so that every reader can learn from the adversity experiences we all went through. Things have been tough in the past, and we truly believe that just because we went through hardships doesn't mean that you have to as well. This book is meant to teach, provide short-cuts, and inspire you whether you are an aspiring entrepreneur or have already been successful at this for many years.

I want every reader to soak up as much education and enjoyment from every co-author here. We are all willing to become vulnerable and open up our lives to the public for the sole purpose of benefiting others who will learn from our experiences. I wish everyone a happy and successful journey through life. Cheers, and enjoy the amazing stories.

We did it, and so can you!

ABOUT ANDREW IZUMI

Andrew is an action taker, an independent thinker, and a leader in high-ticket sales strategies. He loves to help owners of small and medium-sized businesses attract more high-ticket clients, command higher prices, and scale their bottom-line revenues. This is achieved without having to hard-sell clients, use outdated sales strategies, or build complicated sales funnels.

Andrew has been a leading sales manager for over a decade, having achieved certificates like Leading at Emerson, a Fortune 500 company. Some of his past customers served include MillerCoors, Disney Animations, Exxon Mobile, Chevron, Edwards Air Force Base, Port of Long Beach, MGM Grand, and many more. When working with these companies, an ROI (return on investment) was always achieved and was as high as multiple hundreds of thousands of dollars per year after the sale. Andrew is responsible for over $100 million in sales within California alone.

Andrew enjoys working with business owners who are looking to solve their customer's problems and serve them at the highest level. His customer's high-ticket solutions are the driving force behind his service as Andrew loves to see people succeed. Outside of work, Andrew enjoys outdoor hobbies, including fishing, rock climbing, and skiing. He looks forward to connecting and building a great relationship with you.

You can find out more about Andrew Izumi at:
www.highticketmomentum.com

THE POWER OF BELIEVING IN YOURSELF

by Kevin Steven

When it comes to overcoming adversity, I've had a lot of stuff happen to me over my life that I've had to get through and get past. Not only am I a Marine Gulf War veteran, but you can also add to that all of the things that have happened along the way. The one thing that I've learned that's helped me throughout my entire life is that I do not have to be a product of the environment I'm in. I can change things. I may not be able to leave the environment that I'm in, but I don't have to be a product of that environment.

I am not the kid who was raised by my mom. I know that I'm a better person. I know that I'm not what I was told I was my entire childhood. I overcame that obstacle, which was being told I was one thing and learning later I wasn't. The saddest thing that happens to a lot of children is that they become what someone else's opinion or unjust label of them is. I spent seventeen years with my mother. I became a product of what my mother had raised, so going out into the real world, I was this kid who had a false sense of self-worthlessness. One day, I just realized I don't have to be that; I can break this cycle.

To me, overcoming adversity means you can change. You can break yourself of habits that have been ingrained in you over the years. You can choose to do that, and that's what I've done. I chose to break those habits. I knew that I could be better than what I had been told my whole childhood, and this is why I always push for bigger and better. This is why, through my

17

twenty-five years in corporate sales, I was always hungry. I was never going to lose to anybody. I had spent my entire life being told I was never going to get anywhere, that I was never going to be successful, but that was just someone else's idea of me, not mine. I became determined to prove them wrong. That became my goal my entire adult life, and I did it. I was very successful.

After all the success, I had this moment when one day I realized, I'm giving my entire life away. I've lost a marriage. I've lost myself because of this corporate job and the hours I put into it, the travel. I'm trading life, trading hours in my life, all to make the dollar. It didn't add up the way it should. I had come to the realization that I needed to walk away from that world, and that's how I became an entrepreneur.

I launched my first software company in 2016. I've launched several software applications that we have built for ourselves and for other people. We're launching two new applications as we speak. This is how I got introduced to this ClickFunnels world just over a year ago, and that introduction to ClickFunnels is how I got started in the digital marketing space. There was an agency that wanted to bring us on as a customer and try some digital marketing processes out for one of our software companies. However, by the time I signed the scope of work and sent it back to them, they were so busy they couldn't take us on as a client. I was like, well, crap; now what? I had to find out on my own. So I created my ClickFunnels account, and I was like, okay, what does this do? So I started teaching myself. Fast forward thirteen months, and I've gone from what on earth is ClickFunnels to holy crap, what's going on?

If you're new in this space and don't really have the experience, it's very easy to get lost down rabbit holes. Some people get tricked by savvy internet marketers, and unfortunately, there's a lot of this "fake guru" stuff going on out there, gurus who don't really know what they're doing.

There are a lot of people who really aren't customer-based or customer-focused, and they are very new to selling programs. They haven't earned their stripes in an industry to get the experience they need to understand customer experience and how best to serve their customers. You have to ask yourself questions like, is this person legit? You should talk to people, talk to customers they work with, and find out if this person is truly worth their salt.

My goal has always been to over-deliver on everything. I love connecting people. If you have a hurdle in your life, I want to connect you with somebody who can help you get past whatever is holding you back. And that's what I've been doing since I landed in this space. I believe in that methodology of helping someone in their business, finding the answers they need to get them over those hurdles.

I then had to figure out the "passion" part of this business. I mean, whatever your passion might be, how do you monetize that? How do you make that your paycheck? And then discovering the next step in the process: your purpose.

I think you need to lay a good foundation; you need to have the right intent. Your heart has got to be in the right place to get to that purpose. For me, I had a big epiphany when I got involved with Jay Shetty's team. I asked myself, *Is what I'm doing today truly purposeful? Am I changing lives?* And you know, the last thing I ever want to do is not deliver on an offer. I mean, I don't want someone to walk away thinking they wasted their time or money.

If I had to close this chapter with anything in relation to overcoming adversity, it's this: You can be anything you want to be, as long as you're honest with yourself. Don't let others define you.

ABOUT KEVIN STEVEN

Kevin has 25 years of experience in VP sales management. He has launched multiple tech startups in software and SaaS.

Kevin is a connector of people and has closed over 900 million dollars in sales revenue over his career. Thank you for watching this Marine Corps Veteran! OohRah!!!

bit.ly/DigitalImpactStrategies
https://www.facebook.com/airfryerkevin

ESCAPE YOUR 9-5 WITH ONE SIMPLE SALES FUNNEL

by Blake Nubar

My obsession with sales funnels and online marketing began back in 2016. Unknown to me, but it happened out of pure frustration...

At the time, I was working for a fitness company that set out to create programs to teach people how to become personal trainers. We had just finished developing our flagship program called "Hollywood Muscle," and we couldn't wait to get it out for the world to see. Excited, I handed the entire program over to the marketing department, who was responsible for creating the strategy to generate visitors (traffic) and eventually make sales.

At the time, no one had ever heard of a sales funnel or even knew what one was. They were still operating under the notion that websites would get people to take action. They started driving visitors to the site, but nothing happened. No one gave us their email, let alone their credit card. What they were doing was simply not working.

With each day that passed without a single sale, I started to grow frustrated with everything. We just built something, and no one was buying it. I couldn't just sit back and watch our amazing product die a miserable and slow death. We put way too much work into it to not give it a fair chance at succeeding in the marketplace.

One night, as I was browsing Facebook, I was hit with an ad from this guy named Russell Brunson.

"Weird Marketing Experiment to Increase Traffic,
Conversion, and Sales Online!"

It stuck out like a sore thumb among everything else in my feed. So, I did what any person in pain would do—I clicked. I hoped it was the "painkiller" I was looking for to finally start selling our brand-new program online.

The ad brought me to a funnel, which at the time I thought was a website, where Russell was on camera for ninety minutes talking about all of the different ways you can sell your products and services using these things called funnels. I was so hooked from this video that, when it ended, I started it back from the beginning to watch it again. At this point, I knew he had me.

On zero sleep but completely awake and excited, I quickly hopped in my car and shot straight over to the office. I grabbed a marker and headed to the whiteboard wall, where I began doodling out my first iteration of a funnel.

I remember employees walking in looking at me like I was crazy, asking all types of questions as to what I was doing. My response was, "I know how we're going to sell our program. We're going to use a funnel!"

"A funnel?" they asked.

"Yes, a funnel!" I said excitedly.

None of us really had any idea what one was at the time, but that ninety-minute video presentation was enough to get me moving. And after about ten minutes, I had my first version of a webinar funnel completely sketched out.

But this was just the act of marketing I was going to use. It was the framework I thought would be the best to follow to sell our brand-new program online. But there was a big part that was still missing. A funnel is useless if you don't have the meat and potatoes in place. The main ingredients needed to both create and deliver real value to the customer—the sales message and offer.

I called up our partner at the time who was the face of the program we had just created.

"Eric, I need you to record a webinar presentation for me," I said in all seriousness.

"A webinar?" he replied.

"Yes, I'm going to write up a webinar presentation for you, and you need to record it so we can start selling."

He was in. He quickly recorded the webinar and sent it back to me a few days later. We had the sales message, we had the offer, and we had the funnel. And at this point, we were ready to rock and roll.

With everything ready to go, I quickly knocked on the door of the marketing department to let them know it was time to turn on ads to our new sales machine I had just created. Man, I was so excited. It was really cool to see something come to life that just a couple weeks prior didn't even exist.

To really put effort into learning something new, and seeing how it all unfolds, creates a sense of accomplishment regardless if it works or not. The fact that it was now a living, breathing thing with an actual pulse kind of felt like a win in a weird way.

When the ads turned on, people not only clicked to the page, but they were opting in! It was at that moment I committed and believed in this type of system more than ever.

The webinar we structured was a "Like-Live" webinar. It's basically a cool way of saying that it was pre-recorded (remember, I didn't really know what I was doing) but the date on it was a set date in the future so it felt like a live event (one of the take-aways I quickly learned from Russell in that video of his I saw). This was an important concept in order to ensure high show-up rates. It had to feel live.

When the day finally came around, I was nervous. I remember that the entire morning I couldn't really get any work done. All I thought about was whether or not this thing was going to be a success. Was my first funnel actually going to work? Was this going to rake in cash?

By the time the webinar started, I was next-level nervous. I don't care what anyone says, the moment you are *not* nervous when you launch something for the first time is the moment you *should* start to get nervous.

Then something crazy happened…

People actually showed up! We had people sitting down at their computer screens from all over the world, watching as we gave our presentation.

As we progressed, we started approaching the part where we made our offer and asked people to take action. We had to nail this part. It had to come off as confident enough to instill the trust that we truly stood behind what we were selling. We had a great offer, but we knew the only way to validate it was to let people vote with their wallets.

And when the time came to do so…

Nothing happened.

Five minutes, ten minutes, then twenty minutes go by, and finally, the webinar ended.

And not a single person purchased.

I was devastated. I walked out of the building and sat down on the steps that led up to the front doors. Head in my hands, I was defeated. So many thoughts ran through my mind.

Why didn't this work?

I did everything I was told to do.

I remember thinking that this was, once again, another failure. It was another wasted time commitment to a dead-end endeavor.

Or so I thought…

Because after a little time passed, I decided to walk back in and figure things out. During my walk back to my desk, an idea hit me…

What if, I thought. *What if it wasn't quite over yet?*

I went straight to my computer and decided to try something. With my finger hovered over the refresh button, I pressed it. It was all I had at the time, so I figured I'd give it a shot. I didn't know at the time, but the next thing that happened changed my life forever.

SALE.

I couldn't believe it! Someone actually pulled out their credit card and paid us $797? If you could have seen me at that moment, it would have been a funny sight, I'm sure.

I went absolutely crazy in excitement. I'll never forget the name of the person: Bon T. Wherever this person is right now, I wish I could thank her because she had a bigger impact on my future than I could have ever imagined.

This thing, this idea, this funnel "stuff" actually worked! To follow a framework and see it all come together in the way it did with a result-driven ending was the absolute best feeling in the world. I felt like I was on top of the world!

After a few hours after that first sale, you would think the emotional rollercoaster would have died down. But it didn't. What I just experienced changed the trajectory of my life forever. I was so drawn into this world of funnels and captivated beyond belief that I walked into my job the next day and did the unthinkable...

I quit.

I barely had any money saved and no plan, but I knew there was something to this "funnel stuff." There was something to this online money that I knew had the potential that could finally give me the type of freedom I wanted so desperately, the type of freedom that could let me do what I wanted, when I wanted. Even more important, it was the freedom to wake up every day doing something I *loved*.

I gave my two-week notice and immediately started preparing for the next chapter in my life and the incredible journey I was about to embark on.

Why am I telling you this? More so, why should you care?

Since this first encounter with sales funnels not too long ago, I have gone on to generate over $11M in sales, partnered with sharks form ABC's TV Show, *Shark Tank*, worked with HGTV stars, and helped thousands achieve financial freedom using funnels.

I don't say that to posture and peacock. I say that because I want you to understand that *anyone* can do this. No one is born an expert, and if you are willing to put in the work, dedicate the time, and overcome all of the obstacles that will get in your way, you can have any type of business you want using these incredible sales machines.

I am so grateful for what I went through that day because It wasn't until this experience that I fully understood the power behind what a single funnel could mean for your family, your business, and your life.

Some of you are reading this right now and have never launched a successful funnel. Some of you have. Regardless of where you're at with your business, one thing is for certain:

A funnel is your fastest ticket to the life you want. And I'd like to be the person to help you get it.

ABOUT BLAKE NUBAR

Blake Nubar is an entrepreneur in Orlando, Florida. He entered the world of funnels and internet marketing two short years ago and has since helped hundreds of people achieve financial freedom using sales funnels.

In 2017, he co-founded a digital marketing agency that specializes in marketing strategy and funnels. With a keen eye for what "works" and an obsessive passion for design, Blake has been able to achieve extraordinary success for himself and the clients he works within a short period of time.

Holds The Record For Fastest 2 Comma Club Funnel (43 Days)
Helped Clients All Around The World Scale To Millions
Over $10,000,000 In Lifetime Sales Through ClickFunnels
Business Consultant, Speaker, Mentor, & All-Around Good Guy

Join Blake on Facebook at
facebook.com/groups/604206903401089

FUNDAMENTALLY REFRAMING ADVERSITIES

by Akbar Sheikh

Adversity is a skill set; it's just a choice.
You're going to let it own you, or you're going to own it.
It's totally up to you.

—Akbar Sheikh

Whether we have overcome adversity in our professional career, personal life, mentally, or a physical struggle, everybody has a little bit different story. But there's a reason why we're all on this entrepreneurship journey together. What were some of the struggles, potholes, and landmines? What did we have to avoid to get to the stage that we're at today?

This is a very fascinating topic, so let's unpack this a little bit. You meet people who are stuck, and they've been stuck for many years. They've got the same pay level or income level, having the same personal relationships. If you had met them five years ago and wrote down how their personal life was going, their health, their business, and all these kinds of categories, then five years later they're pretty much in the same situation. They've not been able to overcome adversity because adversity is what life throws at you, right?

They are still stuck in their negative thoughts and limiting beliefs. You know, the "Oh, I would only make it if," and "if only this and that," and this holds a lot of people back.

I recently celebrated a successful student moment I'm very proud of. She lives in India, which is considered a developing country or third-world country or what have you. It's a place of extreme poverty in parts. She has dark skin, like me, and she has a thick accent. And she's a Facebook marketer in a very highly saturated market. A lot of people in that position (and I know people like this) would say, "I have an accent, so I don't see how this is going to work," or "I live in in a different area," or "It's a different time zone; it's just not going to work," or "I don't look like them."

There are a lot of people that you don't know warning you about people who are enemies and people who don't have your best interest in this next move. The number one and the bottom line is that your number one enemy, in reality, is actually yourself. People sell themselves something every day. They sell themselves that they are going to make it, or they're not going to make it. Now why I'm so proud of the student? With all the stuff that people use as an excuse, she overcame them all and now has a flourishing Facebook agency. She has one of the world's top agencies, and what's beautiful is that something like this can happen quickly. Her turn around came in the first year we started working together. The mind is the biggest block.

I'll never forget this very interesting moment in time. I used to have a crippling anxiety disorder, and I went through all sorts of therapies, therapists, daily medications, and emergency medications such as Prozac or Xanax. I had counselors, doctors, and all sorts of stuff. I'll never forget when I met one counselor who I was trying to work with.

I caught him in this rare moment like he broke the third wall. It was kind of like, he made a mistake, and he told me something like he was talking to his best friend. He says you can actually cure anxiety like this; you just have to tell yourself and believe that everything's okay. It's very easy to say but very difficult to actually do. But it is a true statement. That reality was life-changing. Anxiety is created by the mind continuously selling itself that something's wrong. The second you do a pattern

29

interrupt, and you insert an idea that everything's working, and you actually truly believe that, everything starts to become okay.

To overcome adversaries is a multi-step process. To overcome adversities, you have to fix yourself first. You need to make sure that you're in good physical shape, make sure you're spiritually healthy, and make sure that you have discovered your "why." Discovering your why becomes your circle of power so the people around you are not negative and bringing you down. These are all powerful things.

I just met a guy who's been in a terrible marriage for many, many years, and he cannot succeed in any aspect of his life because he is constantly surrounded by negative energy. The second you release that energy, everything changes overnight. It really did for me. When you release that negative energy, things can happen very quickly.

I became set to overcome adversities but first needed to quickly take massive action. You need to take a massive sweep, take a look at all your negative influences, and get rid of them. You've got to get rid of all your negative influences in one sweep. You've got to become healthy, get proper rest, drop the soda, drop the meat five times a day, drop all the sugar—drop all these things immediately; drop all your bad habits immediately. Take action, big action, and implement quickly.

Nobody wants to hear this stuff; most people just want a blue-print, a pill, someone to hold their hand and tell them what they want to hear. The reality is that there's always going be someone trying to sell you something. But this is what works. You know, I joke with people, but if you want to build a real business with a strong foundation that can actually give you and your family a high-quality life and impact thousands of people all around the world, all you need to have are some fundamentals in place, and that starts with you. The bottom line is that it's like training. You have to go through things; you have to pay your dues and go through some adversities.

You have to survive something to receive the reward. Just like back in the day, if you wanted to eat well, you had to go hunt.

You had to do something to get that reward, and the reward was eating. You have got to take some action, you've got to have hunting tools, shoes, a sharp hunting stick, a way to get the hunt processed.

There's always going to be something you can sell yourself. The difference between the guys and the guys who've done it, some say is 80% mindset and 20% strategy. I would argue that it's 90% mindset and 10% strategy. The strategy part is not that difficult. I mean, there are a million moving parts for an online business. There are opt-in pages and freebies, or an application page, book, funnel, webinar funnel, copy, ethical principles of persuasion, email, follow up, and checkouts. There are sales and customer service. It can be an overwhelming amount of stuff. It's not that the actual strategy and tactics are that complex; it's mostly, can you believe that's the process?

I've met some people who are crushing eight-figure businesses, and they're not like, how do I say this—they're not super smart. They're not smarter than you or me. In fact, they might even be a little less smart. But they have an elevated mindset, and the best thing you could do is to commit to yourself.

Sometimes my wife gets angry or upset. I'll ask her if she's eaten and she'll reply that no, she's trying to feed the kids. I say, you can't care for other people until you care for yourself first. This scenario is being set up to be a terrible interaction between you and the kids. It's going to be anxious and fighting tension. It's not going to be good at all. It's very important to first take care of yourself to take care of others.

Adversity is going to come. There are good times that you need to learn to enjoy, and then there will always be the bad times that you need to learn how to survive. We've got some hate online, and every business gets hit by the haters, but that doesn't matter how big or small. Whatever you are, whoever you are, everybody gets it.

My student that I mentioned earlier had some hate directed at her course. The complaint was over them being able to Google her content. She let it affect her. She let that baseless trash affect her so negatively that she actually went off the radar for three months. She didn't sell anything for three months.

People who hate are in pain, and then you put your own pain on top of it. That's not a very tasty sandwich. You guys just throw that away and realize that's just humanity. That's why people have bad days. I know some really nice people have had bad days, or they just don't know what they're talking about, or they're just jealous, or they're giving up. And they think that they don't want to blame themselves, so they're blaming you thinking, *Oh, it's not me; it's that your stuff is garbage.* Even though they didn't really do anything, even though they fell through, and even though they didn't commit.

You have to understand that a lot of people are like that. You have to concentrate on the ones who actually implement and the ones who are actually winning. Adversities are going to come every day, and you have to know this as an entrepreneur. You have to maintain a steady baseline, and you can't just dip when adversity comes along. You have to stay in that commitment to you and maintain a high level of productivity. The way to do this is through daily affirmations, positive intentions, constant gratitude, prayer, having a deep understanding of how things work as a whole, people's different behavioral skills to have your eye on the prize, and your mission. You know, these are some of the things that really help keep a constant level of productivity. It's extremely valuable, and you must be able to dive deep.

The biggest adversity I had to overcome within my entrepreneurship journey, has been failure, when things just weren't working. I had so many failed businesses before I figured it out. Every time I felt like quitting, every single time I went to go look for a job, that was something I had to overcome. That, "Hey, you're not employable," or "you can't last at a job." I had to change that to, "You're an entrepreneur," and "you got to figure this out." It's just that kind of "burning the bridge" mentality that I had to adopt.

I'll never forget the moment where I was just like, dude, I don't care. I remember there was a euphoric smile, like, I don't care, I'm going to make this work. There was no other choice. Other people were making it work, and I was going to make it work, too. And here's the thing, I'm just not going to give up because that was my biggest adversity. That was the biggest. It's freaking easy to give up. Easy breezy, that's what my wife says. Easy breezy Japanese lemon squeezy. I guess it's from Australia, but we'll just call say it was my wife saying it for now.

It's easy to give up, and I did so many times because it's just an easy thing to do. But I'll tell you, looking back, I could have made any one of those businesses work if I didn't let the adversary win, if I didn't choose to give up, if I had only chosen to actually stick to it and figure out why it wasn't working, what's my strategy, what are my tactics, how can I do this and what kind of support can I get? If I committed to it, I could have done it. However, I wasn't in a position to do that because I wasn't primed. It hadn't clicked what I call claiming "my real power" yet. My real power is aligning my nutrition, my mentality, and my spirituality. My body has got to be right. My environment has got to be right. You see what I'm saying? That's why giving up was an option for me. Now, it's not even an option.

Here's the perfect example, a TEDx talk. It was a goal of mine. I wanted to get a TEDx talk. I kept saying, "I'm going to make this happen, this is going to happen. I'm 100% convinced I know that this is going to happen."

The first thing I do is that I put it out there. Who can help me out here? I want to know who has connections or whatever. Soon, somebody says, "Okay, look, I like your stuff. I'll nominate you, and I have voting power so I can nominate." She nominates me to the TEDx people, so cool. Well, that audition failed; they rejected it. I didn't even flicker, and this is the part I really want people to kind of internalize. I didn't flicker. No worries. Well, I reached out to them. (There's a reminder here to put your ego in your pocket.) I reached out to them again because they hadn't corresponded. Tell me what I can do better. I want to audition again. They told me what to do, so I did it, auditioned again, and was accepted. It was really that easy.

The truth is, we're like the thing that no one really wants to hear. He said the ones who make it are really just the ones who refuse to give up. I'm talking about trying until it happens. I'm talking about keep working it until it works. For most online businesses that are in my world (and this is a big, bold statement that I'm about to make), it's really hard to impossible not to make something work if you're taking the right actions and not giving up. I've told that statement to some pretty high-end people. I've said to correct me if I'm wrong. Some people have been in the game longer than others, the people who are at that next level. I've done interviews and said this same thing before, and no one has corrected me.

You can have adversaries every day. They're meaningless. You can power right through them; you got to just make things happen. We're entrepreneurs; we're problem solvers. You've got to own that to understand who we are, and if you don't like that, then you should go get a job. You have to understand who you are. If you're an entrepreneur, your part of a rare breed. We're not better than anyone. We're all equal as humans; we're all equal, but we are different. We need to realize that, and we need to take advantage of that. We need to understand our strengths and weaknesses. We need to find support for our weaknesses, and we become stronger when we utilize and leverage that.

One magical moment when the light bulb turned on, I realized that other people in the business were making it—and they were no different than me. That they were normal weirdos just like me. It's kind of like the saying that when you walk toward God, He runs toward you.

People often ask where I get inspiration. If you search for it, you'll find it. I decided to look in the mirror and tell myself that I was going to keep tweaking and adjusting. I was going to keep getting support. I was going to keep making this happen. I gave myself no other option, and that was when I had my first real success online, and it slowly snowballed from there. Once you finally decide to take true ownership over yourself, your business, and your actions, that's when you finally have that awakening: I can do this.

You really can accomplish anything you want, and there is no adversity, meaning there is no limitation. Take a look at Arnold Schwarzenegger. He didn't fit the mold of bodybuilders in his time. He was from Austria, ended up becoming Mr. Universe and Mr. Olympia (several times), and when he wanted to get into acting, they said, "Have you heard yourself talk? You can't even talk properly. You're funny looking. We can't even understand what you're saying," and he then became one of the largest box office heroes in the history of Hollywood. And if that wasn't enough, he then went into politics and became the governor of the fifth largest economy in the world—the State of California.

Enjoy the journey because most of it is just a journey, and there's always going to be something new. There's always going be adversity, but it's how you deal with it. Are you willing to take ownership and push through it or not? Those are the simple questions that can get you to the next level.

My number one suggestion for everybody is to keep giving every day, whether it's your time, your effort, your kindness, your knowledge, or whatever you have. Just give it and give it openly without expecting anything back. Don't give up because your adversities are your test. It's your daily tasks, and you have to pass it every day to win. You're an entrepreneur, you're a problem solver, you're equipped to do it, you can do it, you just have to choose to do it. I wish nothing but the best for you all.

ABOUT AKBAR SHEIKH

Akbar Sheikh is a #1 international best-selling author, speaker, master of the 7 Ethical Principles of Persuasion, has helped 8 funnels hit 7 figures, father, and philanthropist with a concentration on orphans and giving the gift of vision to blind children.

Before he achieved success, he was homeless, overweight, in a terrible relationship, and suffered from a crippling anxiety disorder.

He does what he does because he believes that entrepreneurs are inherently good people who want to make more so they can give to their families, communities, and favorite charities, hence making the world a better place.

Akbar is on a mission to use persuasion for good, helping people break through ethically.

Learn more at **akbarsheikh.com**

REWIRE YOUR BRAIN AND OVERCOME ANYTHING AS AN ENTREPRENEUR

by Gusten Sun

"I haven't failed, I just found 10,000 ways that didn't work."

—Thomas Edison

A late Tuesday night in the middle of nowhere in 2018. It was 2:00 a.m., and I was driving home from the office. I sat in my car and cried my eyes out. I just needed to let everything out, even if nobody could see it. I felt so lost, so confused, and so exhausted at the same time.

Was this the dream I had chased? Did I go through all that adversity just to reach this constant hustle and grind?

This is the story of how I overcame many adversities and still overcome anything by rewiring my brain constantly and completely.

I have a trick I call the 3 Second Rule, but more about that later.

When I was growing up, I thought that if I failed, I was a failure. I thought that if I wasn't perfect, I wasn't good enough. I thought that if I wasn't school-smart, I wasn't actually smart. I attached my self-worth to my performance, and in doing so, I started feeling like I wasn't worth much.

The crazy part is that I wasn't even the worst kid in school, so I wonder what people with lower grades felt like.

By the way, it's no wonder those kids became troublemaker and were a pain in the a$$ for the teachers. That's what you get for punishing a creative person for not being good at sports. That's what you get for punishing a sporty person for not caring about history.

Side rant, I know, but seriously. Here's the problem, and I have a point with all of this. Who needs to know the Pythagorean Theorem or how many presidents we've had since 1765?

Not me. Not a musical artist. Not a social media creator. Not a professional football player. Not a digital marketer.

The list could go on and on, but you get the point. The system is wired to teach the masses but reward only the top performers. "Performers" according to what the system thinks you're good at.

Here's why I deeply care about all of this. I grew up relatively average. Not too poor, but nothing fancy. I have four sisters and three brothers, so it's a pretty big family. My parents never gave us more than we needed, but they always loved us for who we were. They never gave us things on a silver platter. We had to work for what we wanted, and it's the greatest thing they could've ever thought me because that's what the real world looks like.

They didn't say it, but through their actions, they told us, "If you want something, you better go get it because nobody is going to give it to you." Don't get me wrong; we didn't struggle to survive by any means. They fed us, gave us clothes (up until age fourteen when I started working and could buy my own clothes), gave us a roof over our heads, and all the essentials for living.

But if I wanted a phone, I was the one who bought it. A new bike? I was the one who paid for it. My first car? I paid for it.

Everything.

I had to learn how to take care of myself financially, so I learned how to work hard and get a job. The problem was that once I understood that money gave me options, and all I had to do was work longer hours to get paid more, I quickly burned out while in high school. Waking up at 6:00 a.m., going to school, walking from school to my evening job, and getting home at 11:00 p.m. wasn't healthy.

But it was definitely hard work. I definitely "performed." At the age of seventeen, I was a manager at my job and had a team that worked for me, some of who were older than me, and they didn't like it.

At the age of fourteen, I got my first job, and by the age of twenty-one, I had tried it all. I had fifteen different jobs, I was a college dropout, I had three failed businesses, and I was left with nothing. It was the hardest thing I ever had to overcome.

Luckily for me, I had a loving wife who supported me, paid for the rent, bought me food, and worked hard to pay our expenses while I was trying to figure myself out. It wasn't that I couldn't get another job. It wasn't that I didn't know how to make average money and live an average life. I could've done that and said, "It is what it is."

But I hate that saying. Nothing is what it seems, and you always have the power to change it. Even after fifteen different jobs, I couldn't find what I loved doing. I wanted more. I wanted something beyond average. I didn't feel alive, and life felt pretty empty. I felt like I had untapped potential and a hunger for becoming more.

You know that feeling inside of "there has to be more." Or the feeling of "enough is enough." For me, it came to a point where I said, "Enough is enough; I quit."

That was the start of my entrepreneurial journey.

There was only one problem—money. The bills were piling up, and we didn't know how long we could continue like this before we became homeless.

There's a saying that goes something like, "A healthy man has a lot of dreams; a sick person only has one." I think it's the same thing with money. A financially wealthy person will seek a lot of fulfilment from helping others and living life to the fullest, and that's amazing.

But a broke person only wants one thing. Money.

A broke person is so stressed out by the lack of money that nothing else matters. It's all they can think about. When they go to sleep, when they wake up—all the time. That's how I felt, and I was tired of it. I wanted control of my life. Freedom. Options.

It was the worst feeling in my life, and when I couldn't even pay my own bills, and my wife had to take care of me, I felt like a complete failure both as a husband and a man.

It wasn't just that I wanted to make money. I wanted to show her that I was capable of change. I wanted to prove to her that I was the man I said I was. I wanted to give her everything she deserved. The person she deserved. The feeling of living with a man who was confident, able, and powerful enough to build a future for his family.

And I wanted to do it online. I wanted to build a business of my dreams, work from anywhere, be able to spend time with my family when I wanted to, and not have to listen to a boss ever again.

That was only three years ago, and today I've done multiple six figures online, I work from home in a separate office building so I keep some space from the family, and I decide when I want to take a day off. I have what I would call complete freedom.

But it wasn't easy. Let's dive in how I did just that, because maybe that is something you're dreaming about right now. If so, just know that if I can do it, anyone can.

* * *

As I sat there watching YouTube videos, trying to learn how to start my online business, I was having trouble finding out where to start. I had no idea what to sell and who to sell to.

Until one day it hit me. I wanted to help entrepreneurs and business owners scale using social media. That's the future—social media. I identified a niche, got clear on a problem, and started learning about the solution.

And so I launched my first ever business.

I started working for free, got some results, and then decided to start charging for my services. I immediately re-invested everything I made into new books, courses, and coaches who could help me take my business to the next level. Someone who had been there and could guide me along the way.

If there's anything I had learned from my past, it was how to work hard, so the pattern continued. I was so tired of being broke that I would give up everything else besides my business to make it work.

Now, there's both pros and cons to this. At first, I only saw the pros of working hard. I worked seven days a week, every week, every month—all the time. I stopped hanging out with friends. I never spent more than an hour per day with my wife and my daughter., I went all in.

Just to give you an example of how insane it was, in 2017, I had four days off the whole year. One day was the day our daughter was born, although I still brought my laptop to the hospital, and the day after, I was already working out of my bed in the hospital. The other three days I was in Spain and had no Internet connection, so I couldn't do any work.

Why did I work so much? How come I didn't even have Saturdays or Sundays, off? Why didn't I spend more time with my family? Friends?

I had gone from $400/month to over $10,000/month consistently. The money was great, but something was clearly wrong. The big problem in this pursuit of happiness was I forgot about the pursuit of freedom.

This goes back to the performance thing in school. Why did I work so much even after I no longer needed to? I felt very empty. I felt as if I had lost myself in all this high performance and hustle.

And that's when I had my mental breakdown on that late night in 2018 at 2:00 a.m., driving home from the office. More than anything, I was confused about my purpose in all of this, my purpose here on earth.

Remember how I tried fifteen different jobs before I finally started my own business? The whole reason for doing that was to go find my purpose, not to lose myself in the process. Yet, here I was, and I had no idea what I was doing.

Then one day I had a big epiphany, and my life would never be the same again. I was listening to one of my mentors' videos as he talked about business and success principles. He went deep

41

into mindset and how the subconscious works. He explained how every time when he made a little money, he would always find a way to self-sabotage and lose that money. When he lost all his money, he would go make more out of desperation. He would make a little money, then somehow end up at zero again.

He said, "Some of you are not where you want to be yet because you're still holding on to a past identity who doesn't deserve success." This was huge for me. Like HUGE. It hit me like a wrecking ball in my stomach.

Why? Because it was exactly what was wired in my brain from an early age. There was so much garbage I was carrying from my childhood. School. Religion. Society. Friends. Media. Even my parents.

Before I go into that, I want to point out that I received a lot of good things from my childhood and my parents, whom I deeply love, who always did what they thought was best for me. I love my parents to death, and they have shown me so much love. If I hadn't been raised the way I was, I wouldn't be the person I am today.

But there were a few things that held me back from true success and freedom on a personal and professional level. I grew up in a religion that was very conservative. It's definitely changed since then, but when I was a kid, it was very strict. The main focus was on how much of a sinner we are, and the tone in the church was often very sad. I believe the reason for that was to show how much God loves us, even if we're that horrible.

And while I believe in God, and I know He loves us, I also believe that He doesn't sit there on His heavenly throne judging us for how many mistakes we make, as some people made it seem.

This had a huge impact on my self-image, and when you're a kid, you have no idea what it's doing to you. When you say you're a sinner, that becomes your identity, just like when you put a kid in school in special classes and they become that special kid.

People like to put labels on you. They want to categorize you according to how you perform in certain areas. (By "perform," I mean act, behave, talk, and so on.)

My view on life definitely changed when I became a father myself. I know how much I love my kid, so I can only imagine how God loves me. I don't care if my daughter makes a mistake, I don't tell her to feel bad and to feel sorry. I just laugh with her and hug her. I treat her with love. I don't tell her all the rules of living; I live as an example. And while I'm not even a Christian in some religious people's eyes, I love everyone, and I never judge anyone. I don't base my daughter's worth on how she acts, performs, or behaves; I simply show her how much I love her by being with her. It is sometimes quality time over quantity, but that's way better than always being there physically while my mind is elsewhere.

I've always been wired to believe I'm not worthy, and that's why I needed God. Now, I know that I'm perfect just as I am, and that my actions are simply events happening. My mistakes don't define me. I learn from them, grow from them, and become a better person because of them.

I've learned that I'm perfect just by existing, and that I don't need anyone's approval to confirm that. I love me for being me, and for that, I'm whole. I'm not in need of someone else to realize my worth, so I know I don't have to impress anyone.

The reason I'm telling you all this is because I used to build my business as if I were selling *me*. I based my worth as a human being on the results I was able to generate. Even if I had ninety-nine clients who were happy, and only one was not, I still considered myself a failure. I didn't matter if the client didn't do everything perfectly on their side; if the result wasn't perfect, I took the blame.

Don't get me wrong; I believe in taking responsibility. But I don't believe in identifying your worth with your actions. Your happiness with your results. Your fulfilment based on your performance.

You are not your business. You are not your career. You are more than that. You are complete just by existing; what you decide to do as a career is simply a choice of actions and habits. Learning this changed everything for me.

The reason I had broken down so badly and burned myself to the ground was not that I didn't love what I was doing. It wasn't that I didn't feel inspired to work. I worked seven days a week because I loved it.

But it got to the point that is was unhealthy. If I took an hour to rest, even on weekends, I always felt like there was more I could do for my clients. I always felt like I was lazy if I took some time off. I always felt guilty. I let my clients call me Friday nights when they needed something. Saturday mornings were totally fine. I could definitely have the meeting Sunday if that's what they wanted. I completely neglected myself. Just because they paid, I let them buy *me*. I forgot that my business was selling a service, not me as a person.

Going into 2019, I knew I had to make a shift, and so I did. A massive shift that only I could understand at the time. A massive shift that people told me not to do. Late December 2018, I did it. Something I had been wanting to do for a while. I let go of all my clients.

Yes, that's right. I was back at zero. I had to start all over. No income, no clients, no job, no financial security. I had rent to pay at home, an office, two cars, tons of monthly costs from insurance to food to everything you can imagine. Living costs in the thousands and thousands monthly.

Was I scared? Of course, I was. Was I crazy? Of course, I was. Even if it was scary to start from zero, I was also very excited.

But instead of starting at "what do I sell" this time, I started with "who do I want to become?" I started with my brain. I wanted to take back control.

Now, I've never been big into spending money on flashy things like watches and clothes, and I'm not saying that's stupid if you want to do that. But I've always loved investing in myself. Growing my skills and knowledge around marketing. I knew if I could get results for others, I'd always be able to make money. And it worked.

After working with online entrepreneurs who were just getting started to become *the* funnel builder in multiple seven-figure online businesses, I've proven that it's working. People are paying me big dollars for helping them with such an important skill.

But while growing your skills is important, it's not the most important skill. There's something more important, and once you focus on this, everything else will become easy. It's called "objective thinking," and helps you see events as events with no emotions attached.

You see, when a client gives you honest feedback and isn't satisfied, instead of thinking objectively how you can fix it, your brain instantly goes into the subconscious brain and finds a past event to link with. Once it finds a similar event, it'll spark a negative reaction and reflect a negative emotion that now becomes your action. If you get mad at the client, that's why. If you start feeling like a failure, that's why. If you get scared of meeting them next time, that's why. There's something in your past that is holding you back.

The good news is that the brain is just a computer. It couldn't care less. So, when something bad happens, it's a code that it registers for future references. This means we can insert new positive charges to start rewiring our brain for success. This means you can go back and find the negative charges so next time there will be no gut-wrecking reaction because your dad told you that you suck at football.

If your girlfriend leaves you, there will be no past event in your brain to link to, even if you've had other relationships go wrong in the past, because you've cleared them out.

If you start a business and it fails, you won't be embarrassed to talk about it with friends and family because you know it's just a step closer to your goals. If they don't believe in you, it doesn't matter because you know you're already amazing for who you are and you focus more on your journey than the end result.

Imagine if you could just enjoy life even when nothing's going your way. Imagine if you could laugh and say, "This is going to make me so much stronger moving forward."

Once I started looking at things as events, not a result of my identity, I instantly found my purpose. I used to think my purpose was changing the world, and that once I did, I would've fulfilled my purpose. Once I realized I was perfectly imperfect, and that this season in my life was happening for a reason, I started living in my purpose.

When I spend time with my family, that's my purpose. When I hang out with my friends, that's my purpose. When I work out or meditate, I'm living and breathing purpose.

I am purpose. It's not something to chase. It's here right now, so enjoy it. It sounds so simple, yet it's so hard.

I grew up completely attached to my results, and it almost killed me from burning out. The pattern starts when you're young, and it doesn't stop until you stop it. In my soccer team, I would base my worth on the number of goals I scored. With my friends, I would base my worth on the level of popularity I had.

We're raising our kids to become 'school-smart,' and when you have a weakness, you're told to study that spot a little more so you can raise it to the level of expertise in other areas. In my opinion, we should let kids use their gift to their advantage and excel in that area which they already love to execute in.

Some kids are naturally more street-smart, and they know how to communicate. Some kids are nerdier, and they love solving problems in a math book. Children are wonderfully different, yet we try to level their performance in each category so they can all fit into the same box.

What if we didn't grade people based on their performance but instead on the level of their attitude? What if we would love ourselves and others for who we are, not what we do? Would we use the word success differently? Would people be able to follow their dreams, and simply enjoy the journey? Would we be able to live in complete purpose and stop chasing it?

I know I did, and it changed everything for me. My goal is for it to do the same for you.

Much love,
Gusten

ABOUT GUSTEN SUN

Gusten Sun is an international business and sales funnel consultant featured in major publications such as Entrepreneur magazine, Inc, Buzzfeed, Future Sharks, Thrive Global, and many more.

After successfully building a local social media marketing agency in Finland, he started getting recognition internationally and has now become the go-to sales funnel builder and consultant for entrepreneurs who wants to monetize their expertise and achieve complete freedom online.

Gusten works with entrepreneurs who want to launch or scale an online course, coaching program, or high ticket offer where they don't trade their time for money but want to build an #EducationEmpire to impact the world positively.

Besides business, Gusten is happily married to his wife, Jennie, and is the proud father to his daughter, Neliah. When he's not working, he's living life, spending time with his family, enjoying a BBQ or playing FIFA with his homies.

At the end of the day, he loves building, creating, and changing people's lives through online businesses.

If you want more free tools and training,
go to **www.gustensun.com**

FROM FREELANCER TO ENTREPRENEUR

by Chris O'Byrne

Although I have overcome many adversities in my life, I chose to focus in this chapter on overcoming the adversity of a poor mindset. I grew up in a very traditional farming community where you were expected to either work on the family farm or find a job in the city and work there until you retired. I was in my late 30s before I even realized it was possible to start my own business, and when I finally did several years later, it was more by accident than on purpose.

I officially started my "career" as a freelancer in 2009. I wanted to escape the 9-to-5, having worked as a chemical engineer and high school science teacher for several years. For a couple of years, I had tried to make a go of web design, affiliate marketing, and anything else I could think of, but in 2009, I attended a workshop on editing and became a freelance editor right then and there. And it worked!

As a freelance editor, I made enough to get by on. One day, one of my clients asked if I could create an ebook for her. I said sure, and then quickly jumped on Google and figured out how to do that. I also taught myself how to make covers. Then someone asked me if I could design a print book for them, and once again, I hopped on Google and learned.

Now, I was earning a living as a freelance editor and as a freelance book designer. Business was good, but it soon became too much. I couldn't keep up with the work. I did the math and realized that if I hired someone to handle the design for less than

I was paid by the author, I could make money without doing much more than project management. Sweet!

Soon, I had a cover designer and a print book designer, while I handled the editing, ebook design, and project management myself. And somewhere along the way, I realized that I was building a business and wasn't only a freelancer anymore. The problem was that I only knew how to send invoices and do the work; I didn't know anything about building a business. Once again, I got on Google and started learning.

BECOMING AN ENTREPRENEUR

Systems

The first resource I found was a book called *The E-Myth Revisited* that taught me how to create systems. I started creating and documenting systems, which helped both with training new contractors and with maintaining a certain level of quality. I kept improving the systems, which improved our quality and reliability, and the business continued to grow.

I continued to read books about how to build and run a business.

Today, I have twelve people on my team, including three full-time project managers, several designers, and a marketing manager. Not only is my company growing, but it's growing exponentially. I even hired a business coach last year, which propelled the business even faster.

Most of our systems are documented in Basecamp, the software we use to manage our projects. We created templates for each type of customer, and each template has a few hundred items in a checklist format along with text to explain certain steps. We use templates in our design as a starting point, and that is another form of system documentation. We also use templates for many of our email responses, which saves us a lot of time and keeps us from forgetting important information to share with our prospects and customers. We even have systems for training new team members.

Finances

While creating and documenting systems was the first and probably most important step to creating a real business and becoming an entrepreneur, I still had more to learn. The next step was to learn about finances.

For the first three years, I sent invoices via PayPal and didn't keep track of my income or expenses. It was mostly just me doing the work, and because I was still thinking like a freelancer, it didn't seem to matter. My first big step was to start using an accounting program so that I could track all of the money and also send professional invoices. The accounting software I chose, and still use, is Freshbooks.

I also wanted to learn more about small-business finances, so as I usually do, I found books that helped me. I read about accounting so I could understand which reports I needed to create and analyze. *The Accounting Game* is a simple yet easy-to-understand book that will get you up to speed on basic accounting principles. I also found a book called *Small Business Finance for the Busy Entrepreneur*. However, two of my favorite finance books are *Simple Numbers, Straight Talk, Big Profits!* and *Profit First*. Those two books alone will give you most of the financial education you need.

Marketing and Sales

Although I had a fairly decent background in marketing and sales because I used to be a sales engineer in the paper industry, I knew I still had a lot to learn. Although I have over 100 books related to marketing and sales, my favorite sales book is *The Only Sales Guide You'll Ever Need*. That book really is the only one you'll need for sales, although I'm sure you'll pick up plenty of decent information from other sales books.

For marketing, two of the best books I've found are *DotCom Secrets* and *Expert Secrets*. Another book soon to be released by Steve Larsen is called *Your Core Offer*. Most people have no clue how to create offers, and Steve is an expert at this.

There are so many great marketing books that you'll learn something useful from almost any of them, but the potential for information overload is huge, so I recommend you choose one or two people who have proven themselves and then limit yourself to learning from them.

Part of achieving success with marketing and sales is becoming adept at copywriting. Although you can hire great copywriters, it's worth having a solid understanding of good copywriting so that you can apply the principles and techniques to many areas of your business, such as email copy, landing pages, etc. Two copywriting books I recommend are *How to Write Copy That Sells* and *Copywriting Secrets*.

Networking

For far too long, I avoided networking. I was a lone wolf, and I thought I could create a great business on the merits of my work alone. But once I started attending events and reaching out to people with only the intention of being helpful and useful, my business started to grow fast. A great book in this genre is *Never Eat Alone*. However, books alone won't work here. You need to get out there and meet people. Social media is a good start, but don't limit yourself to the online world. Get out there and meet people in person!

There are many great conferences and events, and there are more popping up all the time. Some of the big events are Social Media Marketing World, Funnel Hacking Live, and Traffic and Conversion Summit. But don't limit yourself to the big conferences. My best connections and partnerships have been made by attending small "mastermind" events where there might be ten to thirty people.

And speaking of masterminds, look into joining a paid mastermind group. Most of these cost in the neighborhood of $500 per month, but they're well worth it. There might be eight to ten people in your mastermind group, and they are usually led by someone who has already achieved the success you're looking for. Not only do you get their personal attention, but you also have the opportunity to learn from and teach a small group of similarly minded people. These are powerful experiences, and you will probably develop life-long friendships.

Last, get a coach. I hired an expensive but excellent coach last year, and not-so-coincidentally, my business grew exponentially. Not only did I learn valuable information, but I also connected personally with a very successful entrepreneur. He, in turn, connected me with many other successful entrepreneurs, which then resulted in many new partnerships and business opportunities.

SUMMARY

As I learned in *The E-Myth Revisited*, I learned how to become an entrepreneur when I changed my focus from working *in* my business to working *on* my business. This advice has become cliché, but it's still true. I didn't just stop working in my business; it was a process of slowly doing less as I hired more team members. Today, I spend most of my time creating partnerships and doing business development. I still read voraciously and never stop learning.

For me, the process involved learning about systems, finances, sales, and marketing, and then getting out there and meeting people I could help, even if it didn't directly result in business. My focus was on the other person, not my own potential gain, and that is the key to successful networking and partnerships.

ABOUT CHRIS O'BYRNE

Chris O'Byrne's mission is to help you change lives, build your brand, and grow your business by writing and publishing a life-changing book—or booklet. And it's much easier than you think!

Learn more at **jetlaunch.net**

MASTERING LIFE AND ITS UNEXPECTED INGREDIENTS

by Faith Sage

August 13, 2014 was one of the best days and worst days of my life. Let me explain.

I secured this pretty sweet gig. I was the new head pastry chef for a private country club. Not too bad since I had just graduated Le Cordon Bleu with my associate's degree in Patisserie and Baking a mere three months before.

I loved my job. I was able to arrive and leave whenever I wanted to. I had no restrictions on what type of food I could buy. And I had free reign on what desserts I could make. Heck, I even got permission to create a pastry table at their holiday buffets.

Life was good.

Enter the head chef: a wisp of a man with an attitude the size of Canada. He didn't like his authority being challenged or his cooking skills or his popularity. He was mean, and he created unsafe working conditions regularly. No one would stand up to him—until me.

Things had been heating up between us for several weeks and not in a good way. We were constantly at each other or ignoring each other. Definitely not a healthy working relationship for either of us or the other chefs in the kitchen.

But on this day, I decided to do something different.

I decided to walk away and let him have the club. I wasn't angry. I wasn't doing it for spite. I was just tired of the angst and turmoil that our spats were causing in me and in the kitchen as a whole. Plus, he had been there way longer than me. So, I put my notice in.

I went home that night and searched for "work from home jobs that aren't a scam." I literally typed those words in my search engine, and I read through the mail gigs, the secret shopper gigs, the send-a-letter gigs. I thought I was completely wasting my time and was just about to give up when I ran across American Writers & Artists, Inc. (AWAI) Six-Figure Copywriting program.

Intrigued, I clicked the link and snagged their report, putting myself on their list. That was the day I began my journey to become the next top copywriter.

Only one problem.

I actually had to do the work. I had to buckle down and go through the program.

Just a side note... With a husband in the military and raising a blended family of seven, time was decidedly not my friend.

But I was determined to do this. I was determined to change the course of my life and the lives of my family. As parents, we want more for our children than what we had.

When I received an email about their upcoming Copywriting Bootcamp to be held that October, I knew I needed to be there. I needed to surround myself with these people in the hopes that all their knowledge would rub off on me. That I would magically gain the piece of the puzzle I was missing. I reserved my spot.

I received an email telling me what to expect at the bootcamp—the speakers, how to get the most out of the event, dress code, breaks—you know, the usual. Except, at this bootcamp, they have what's called a job fair where they have tables and tables of businesses and companies looking for copywriters. You can submit your spec work ahead of time, or you can chat with them at the event.

Obviously, it's way better to submit your work ahead of time, but I didn't have time for that nor did I understand how to do copywriting very well. As I read that email, it also stated that having a website would set you apart from the rest of the newbies coming in. Naturally, I set about getting a website.

There was just one problem: I didn't have any extra cash laying around for that, nor did I know anyone who built them.

I did the next best thing; I began the daunting task of building my own WordPress website.

At first, it was a little tough, but I picked up on the language pretty quickly and had my site built and ready to go when I went to the bootcamp just two short months later. I even going so far as to switch from wanting to be a copywriter to wanting to become a web designer and builder.

On the twenty-six-hour drive home from the bootcamp with my two daughters, all I could talk about was copywriting and building websites.

By 2016, I was still not achieving the type of success I had been reading about. *"Make 6 figures as a copywriter in less than a year."* I felt I was missing something, but I had no clue what it was. With pressure from my husband and family to get a real job and make some money, I caved.

I took a job laying pavers and building retaining walls. The money was great, but by the time 7:00 p.m. rolled around, I was out. This left me little time to continue pursuing my freelancing dreams, so I put them on ice to bring in some kind of income.

Then, August 10, 2016 hit. It was the day I received the phone call that our nineteen-year-old daughter had been killed in a vehicle accident.

My world STOPPED!

Instantly.

I was so focused on the loss of her and keeping our family together that I didn't really grieve. I compartmentalized all the feelings and emotions so I could just be there for my family and not fall apart. And it worked—or seemed to, I thought.

I began just going through the motions during the day and crying myself to sleep at night. My weight began ballooning again, and I was at my all-time heaviest. I had contained the feelings and emotions so much that they were always brimming at the surface just waiting to spill over.

And then they did—months later.

When the tears finally consumed me, I was able to release the anger, the fear, even the rage—all the pent-up emotions that were threatening to collapse me.

The healing process had finally begun. I began dreaming again. I began doing again.

In 2017, I purchased a ClickFunnels subscription to check it out. I was building landing pages on another platform but didn't like how clunky it was. At first, it was difficult and time-consuming, but I was making progress.

Honing my skills, diving deep into copywriting, and building websites, I was reminded of how much I loved both of them. Of how I craved success by freelancing.

I also realized how fragile and short life can really be, and it changed me. It changed the way I think and the way I do business.

You might be thinking, "Wow, that's a rough ride, I'm so glad you finally made it." But I still hadn't made it yet. I was still playing it safe. I was still holding onto the "what if it doesn't work out?" card. I was clinging tightly to my life jacket but dreaming of the deep end.

In 2018, I took off the life jacket and dove straight in. I had signed up for ClickFunnels and attended their Funnel Hacking Live event. It changed my world. I was tired of the limitations I had placed on myself and decided there is no other way but to go all in.

One of my favorite quotes from Tony Robbins is, "If you want to take the island, you have to burn the boats." Meaning, if you want to succeed with anything in life, you have to commit to going all in. If you leave yourself a way out, you're not fully committed, and therefore, you'll always have in the back of your mind, *Oh well, I'll just do XYZ it doesn't work out.*

That's the wrong mindset to have. And that was the key piece I was missing in the very beginning. The mindset.

For me, there is no other way. I am all in, and I design and build sales funnels.

ABOUT FAITH SAGE

Faith began her freelance journey in August of 2014 after a run-in with her head chef. She soon realized that the job would never lead her to her dreams and was only causing angst and chaos within her. The long commute and the time away from her family of seven didn't help, either.

So, she set out to find another way to help her family financially and stumbled upon sales copywriting.

Knowing nothing about business, marketing, or freelancing, she studied hard to understand this new world by attending conferences, masterminds, and meetups. Using her newfound knowledge as a springboard, she quickly found clients eager for her services writing sales copy, designing websites, and building sales funnels.

For more information about Faith and to get a FREE copy of her $97/month newsletter, The Funnel Manifest, head over to **www.faithsage.net/free-newsletter**

GUTTER 2 GLORY
WHEN YOU'RE AT THE BOTTOM,
THE ONLY PLACE TO GO
IS THE TOP

by Matt Rodak

"You are worthless, you will never become anything, and you will never be anything!" Those words have been in my mind for so many years. There is not a day that goes by that I do not think of them, and the day they were spoken over me by one of my teachers in front of the class. You see, it is not just once a day I think of them, but multiple times a day those words run through my head and across my thought process.

I grew up in a Midwestern, blue-collar, lower-middle-class town with a hard-working family. During my fifth-grade year, my parents got a divorce that shook my world to its core. The divorce, like most, was very bad. There was tremendous phycological trauma done to me that left me withdrawn and not sure how to act around my family. Even though my family loved me and always wanted the best for me, I did not know how to interact with them as I once did.

Years after the divorce, and going into high school, I started to find my new self in gangs and the gang culture. I found that gang life and my new friends all had some pretty deep stuff in common. None of us had a good home life, none of us had any vision of going to college, none of us had any type of real plan for the future.

While in high school, I was not a good kid. I skipped class, got into fights, and did whatever I wanted whenever I wanted. Going to school was more of a social thing and a way to make extra money. I really hated it and found no reason to go since I had zero plans for college. In fact, the school told me I did not even have to take SATs or ACTs (I'm not even sure what the difference is), so I didn't. Eventually, I had gotten into too many fights, and the last straw was trying to use a small bat in a fight (in my defense, there were six guys versus me). The school had sat me down with my dad and told us to our faces that the school would be much better off without me there. A week prior, I had been told I was worthless, and with that in my mind, I dropped out.

As a dropout, I had nothing going for me. I had no diploma and no trade or skill except selling drugs, which no one was advertising for that at the moment. I ended up falling into depression and making some very bad choices that lead me to pursue my street career. I started selling more drugs and started to make a fairly good amount of money for my age.

At this point, I thought that I was just going to be a drug dealer, and that would be my legacy. One day, my grandmother asked me what I was doing and how everything was going. I told her not good and let her know some info about what I was doing. She encouraged me to go, and at least get my GED. Since it was my grandmother, I decided to honor her request. I went back, studied, and got my GED.

After I earned my GED, I thought, what the hell, maybe I should go to college. I started to get interested in business and how business works, but I had no idea where or how to find out more. One day, I saw an ad for a degree in entrepreneurship in some town in Iowa. I called and scheduled an appointment. Not knowing what to expect, I drove the six hours there and met with a nice lady.

At the college, I received a tour of the campus and was shown all of the amenities to make my choice that much easier. While going on the tour, I remember feeling completely uncomfortable and feeling like I did not belong because *You are worthless, you will never become anything, and you will never be anything!* I felt ashamed and asked to return to the office to finish the process. Upon walking into the office, we started to discuss the degree for entrepreneurship. I asked about the classes, and when I looked at them compared to the traditional business degree, there were only two classes that were different. The two classes that were different were how to think like a business owner, classes one and two. That was it; there was no other difference between the degrees.

I asked about that, and the lady's response was that, to become a good entrepreneur, you need those classes and a degree. Now, this was 1998, and I knew you did not need a degree to become successful. I expressed my thoughts and was told I was wrong. I sat back in my chair, looked at the lady, and said, "No, you are wrong." Before this, I had no real proof, no real hard evidence that she was right or wrong other than my gut feeling. I simply got up and walked out and made the trip back home.

On the way back home, I had a fire lit inside of me to show everyone I would be a success and that I would make it. At that time, I had no idea how or where to start. I just knew the fire deep inside was lit, and it was lit with a fierce flame.

Once back home, I tried to think of all the ways to become a success, and all I came up with was selling drugs to get money to start a business. With that, I went full force into the drug game. I ended up getting noticed by some guys who I looked up to and desired to be like because they had businesses, had money, cars, homes, and all that you would think of that someone would have who made it.

After a while of working for these guys, my eyes were opened to what their whole business was about. I found a new desire to become a success in the criminal world. My business took off, and I was making a ton of money and learning a lot about business, both legal and illegal.

By the time I was twenty, I was part-owner of a bar, and by the time I was twenty-one, I owned a nightclub as well. Some of my other businesses included a snow cone stand, a fish fry stand, car detailing, car sales, construction, lawn care, and a restaurant business. I was living a crazy life that most people only saw in movies and on television. I had a ton of money, power, and influence in the city even though I was young. I carried myself like a middle-aged businessman determined to close a new deal except my real business was not a deal that could be negotiated out in the open.

Living this life had placed me in a very unique position where I learned more hands-on about business than going to school and getting a degree. Yes, I made illegal money, but I also had to have legal businesses as well to support my real business. Even though I was in a business that was highly illegal, I was still learning business by trial and error. I had to learn the hard way, and that not only grew my desire to become an entrepreneur, it also drove me to become even more successful.

The skills I learned cannot be taught in school, and they cannot be tested on in a final. I discovered things that no one was talking about that are essential in every business, such as how to read body language, how to listen for the slight change in voice tone, how to negotiate as if your life depended on it, (I saw this type of negotiating with my own eyes), how to start a business from the ground up, and the essential steps to take. I learned about partnerships, LLCs, marketing, advertising, and even how to find out all of the information needed from your competition before the Internet.

I did all of this with, *"You are worthless, you will never become anything, and you will never be anything!"* going through my mind. I finally thought I had made it. I had anything and everything I wanted, I had power, I had success—but not for long.

One day, I was going to hang out with friends when I received a call from a DEA agent who wanted to "talk." I made a beeline to my lawyer and found out that my boss and the other guys had been arrested and were trying to use me as the scapegoat. One day, one phone call, and one bad choice now made me go back to *"You are worthless, you will never become anything, and you will never be anything!"* I had felt as if I were on top of the world, but now the world had crumbled, and I was falling.

I found out that I was potentially looking at a conspiracy charge for narcotics. This means I was not caught with anything, did not get arrested with drugs on me, did not get arrested with money, or anything like that. It simply meant that they connected me to the organization, and that was it. To make it worse, my boss, for whom I would have done anything, claimed I was in charge.

During this time, there was a lot going on, more than I can mention here, but in short, my life had turned upside down. I ended up being in a waiting process of literally waiting on the fed's next move as to what they were going to do. During this time, my life changed again, but for the positive.

I became a Christian and gave my life to Jesus. Before anyone says anything, this is my personal story, and I can never ignore or deny what happened to me. If this offends you, I will not apologize as I would not ask you to apologize for *your* story.

While becoming a Christian, there were many miracles that happened where my legal team was baffled as to what was going on. I told them I was free and did not care what happened because of my new faith. I stopped everything and changed my entire life then and there. I got a real job and started to live as much of a normal life as I could, given the situation.

About eight months after the original raid, I received a phone call from one of the agents who had raided me. I told him to call my lawyer, and he said he did not have to. When I asked what he meant, he said to keep living my new life because they had a new person to follow. He hung up, and I called my lawyer, who called the agent, and they said that they were not going to charge me.

That day changed everything, and I realized I had been given a second chance at life. I decided to go in a completely different direction and help people as much as I could. I enrolled in respiratory school to become a respiratory therapist. During this entire time, the same phrase, *"You are worthless, you will never become anything, and you will never be anything!"* kept popping up, but it was getting quieter.

After ten years in the medical field, I decided to help even more, and I started my own respiratory clinic focused on the skilled nursing facility setting. I grew the company and had over thirty facilities. I also ventured out and started a pizza chain and also became a GNC franchisee. All the while with *"You are worthless, you will never become anything, and you will never be anything!"* in my mind.

That phrase slowly turned into motivation rather than damnation in my future. I have come from the bottom where no one would have ever placed a bet on me making it. I come from a place where every card was against me, but I looked forward and never gave up. I may have made some bad choices on how I got there, but it all worked out for the best, and each thing in my life made me who I am. I would never change anything, and I would never take anything back.

I am now focused on two businesses. One is Best MedEd, where we teach healthcare workers how to create and sell their won knowledge through an online course. The other business is my passion for helping as many people as I can through my base company, Gutter 2 Glory.

No matter what you go through, no matter where you come from, and no matter what someone says, you control yourself and your choices. I made a choice to follow Christ in my own life. I made a choice to use my knowledge from the street in real business to make me who I am. I made a choice to help as many people as I could go from Gutter 2 Glory. Remember, *"You are not worthless, you will become whatever you want, and you will become someone amazing!"*

ABOUT MATT RODAK

"You are worthless and will never amount too anything!" Those were the words yelled at Matt in school from his teacher that would change his entire life and set him on a crazy journey. Matt started his entrepreneur journey as a member in a criminal organization. He owned several businesses, both legal and illegal.

Eventually life caught up, Matt was under investigation, his friends turned on him, and he hit bottom. Matt eventually gave it all to God and decided to change his life. After some time, charges were never actually brought up due to lack of evidence.

That was over twenty years ago, and he has since changed his entire life, giving back and starting over eighteen businesses across various markets and industries from GNC franchise stores, pizzerias, an MMA gym, a medical diagnostic company, and a pulmonary rehabilitation company. Matt is a licensed and registered respiratory therapist with a bachelor's in healthcare administration.

Matt is also an author with multiple guest spots in various marketing and business books as well as a public speaker. He used all his knowledge, both from the street and from traditional business, to build his empire. His passion to help others is like no other and he has helped to change the healthcare industry for the better.

I want to extend an offer to you for taking the time to read my story and making a choice to better your life no matter where you are at. Go to **www.gutter2glory.com** now to claim your free self-assessment and goal guide. I also have an amazing coaching package for you as well just for reading this book and my chapter. My goal is that you become a success and never let anything hold you back.

BREAKING AWAY FROM THE NORM: HOW I ESCAPED THE 9-TO-5

by Kathy Walls

Growing up, I knew I wanted more than just getting a job and barely getting by. I think we all have those dreams and aspirations at some point. I grew up in a single-income home due to my father's heart disease crippling him to the point he could not actively work, so the burden of the home fell on my mother's lap. That struggle is something I knew I never wanted.

To this day, my mother will tell you that I was a more of an "out of the box" thinker and very determined to make something of myself. Not that my other siblings didn't do the same, but I always thought differently. I knew what I wanted from a young age: I wanted to go to college, live in a big town, become a doctor (because I was naive and wanted to be financially secure), marry someone financially stable, and not have kids for a long time. Guess how many of those things actually came true. You guessed it—NONE!

I met my husband when I was 16 years old, married him at age 18, and bought our first home when I was 19. He is only two years older than me, and we worked our asses off to make sure we had plenty of everything. He, too, didn't want to be without, and we knew that with hard work and determination, we could have the world. We both missed out on college, and then three years later, we had our first miscarriage, and that started the need and want for a family. We were blessed with a baby boy a year later followed by a baby girl some 19 months later. We were fulfilled and blessed and broke.

We became a single income family because having two small children and having no education beyond high school made it difficult to get daycare cheaper than the paychecks I would have brought home. We went from being financially stable to draining the savings account. To top things off, I had suffered the passing of my father three days before my daughter was prematurely born. We were in a rut, a sour place, and we didn't know how to dig ourselves out.

My husband tried many things that he had seen on TV. You remember the Don Lapre-era of late-night television. You can make a million dollars if you just buy my course and blah, blah, blah. He was a shiny box seeker, but it was due to wanting more for our family. We tried everything under the moon, and I finally got sick of it. I told him no more; we had to figure something else out. We need to pave our own way, so we did.

As a side hustle, Scott, my husband, installed bag cellular phones in vehicles for a local cellular carrier. I helped him with scheduling appointments, billing, and growing his business until one day it outperformed his 9-to-5. Then, we wondered how much it would take to become an authorized agent for this cellular carrier so we could incorporate the two. One thing led to another, and we found the funding to become an agent and had our first true brick-and-mortar business.

It took some time, but we ran that thing like a well-oiled machine. We were in our mid-20s at that point with two small children and grew the business to over a million dollars in sales. What an accomplishment! We were finally back to where we wanted to be—until the business started taking over our lives. We didn't know what to do because the business was outgrowing us and taking a toll on our well-being and relationship. We worked around the clock and barely saw each other. We argued and could only talk business, and Scott missed out on a lot of the kids during that time due to working extremely long hours. We thought surely this wasn't what success looked like, or at least we hoped that wasn't what it looked like.

After struggling to find balance and getting our bearings, we hit another blow. The agents were being phased out, especially the ones doing better than the corporate stores. Once we saw what was about to happen, we sold out and moved back home. Once again, we were at ground zero, but this time, we had no home. We had to find a rental and start all over again back in our home town.

Scott decided to take on a job as a tile layer, and later, I decided to take a job in a tax office. In fear of not being able to make enough, I enrolled in college. I got a degree in business while taking care of my family and working crazy hours, especially during tax season. It wasn't what I loved to do, but it was something I was good at. I actually hated the work, yet I went $55,000 in debt to secure a future for my family. Makes perfect sense, right?

During the next few years, Scott started his own tile and hardwood installations business, and I continued the tax job. One day, one of Scott's clients asked him if he could print on a tile. In Scott's true nature, he said, "Let me find out." He did some digging and found a process called sublimation. He bought about $10,000 worth of equipment, programs, and product. We studied the process, and so began our ecommerce journey.

We started our ecom journey naively. I didn't understand SEO, online advertising, websites, etc. Hell, I didn't understand online business at all. But I took the helm and decided that it was something I was going to make work so I could quit my 9-to-5 job that I hated so much. The people were great at work, but I was extremely unhappy. I needed out, and I was going to figure out sublimation if it was the last thing I did.

I started by finding free images to re-use and sell on products. I then decided to find a place to buy images that could be used for resale. With the help of my young son and YouTube, I learned how to use graphic design software such as Photoshop. I bought books on how to start an eBay store, and I started following and buying courses on SEO. I was in the hole at this point, but I didn't let that stop me. It was going to work. Well, at least I believed it was going to work.

I started our eBay store and placed listings on it, and tinkered with the product listing and pictures in hopes that I would be found and sales would take place. It was around October, and I knew that I had to get something rolling because another tax season was about to be thrust upon me, and I just couldn't do yet another tax season—but I did.

I didn't understand why I wasn't making the sales like I wanted. I didn't understand why people would look at my items and pass by them. I just didn't understand, and I gave up. We left the equipment in a locked room, and I worked over seventy hours a week for four months yet again for another tax season. I was devastated, broken, and stuck.

After enduring another dreadful tax season, I opened the door to our printing room, and sat on the floor and sat in the quiet for a couple hours. I told myself I knew that thousands of people make a go of this business, so I should be able to do the same. What was I missing? What did I need to do to make this damn thing successful? What, what, what!

Each night after work, I sat down at my computer, and I researched the sublimation and print-on-demand markets. I researched everything from product, designs, platforms, SEO, advertising, etc. Anything that had to do with the business I was trying to create I learned and watched. I took pages and pages of notes, and then after a couple months, I revamped my eBay store, opened an Etsy store, and started social media marketing. Lo and behold, it happened! Sales started coming in, and I finally had activity day after day, week after week, and month after month. It finally came to the point where it was costing me to go to work, so I happily put in my notice. I was free—or so I thought. I may have put in my notice a bit too soon.

What? I know you are saying: "Ah, man, I thought she finally figured it out, and that is why she is writing this chapter." I did end up figuring it out, but way later than where I am in my story. I quit my job without the constant flow of income that exceeded my checks. I hit it twice in the middle of summer, and I thought I was good to go, but I wasn't. I had to constantly figure out what was what in the ever-changing economy. I had to figure out what worked for my type of business and what didn't. I did this alone because I didn't know there was such a thing of a mentor for my type of work.

You know that saying that is going around "burn your boat," and the meaning behind that? If not, let me tell you. When you try to go out and do something on your own, you burn your boat by getting rid of that safety net. For many of us, it could be a 9-to-5 job, it could be a person that enables us in the wrong way, or just something that has us one foot in the door and one foot out. I burned my boat by leaving my job. I had to figure stuff out because I was in a sink-or-swim scenario, and I am so glad I was. Who knows, if I had not burned my boat, I might not be here writing this chapter. In fact, I can guarantee I wouldn't be here because I would have given up and gone back to work.

As I said before, I researched everything related to my business. I had sales, and I had them consistently, but what I didn't have was volume, and my products were all over the place. I didn't have a niche, so I was selling anything I could just to get the sales. It wasn't until I picked a niche that my sales started flourishing. I was able to pick platforms that made sense to me, which eliminated the very first platform I sold on: eBay. I upped my game on social media and honed my Etsy skills.

Once I began social media marketing and really studying the platforms I was selling on, my business flourished to the point that I had to hire help. I had arrived! I made it back to running a full business out of my home, and it grew so big that I even rented office space so we could do our work more efficiently. I expanded my reach and narrowed my niche, and I was making things happen. It wasn't always sunshine and rainbows, but I finally found my calling. I was making well over six figures on Etsy alone, not to mention other places where I was selling my designs.

Finding success was not easy, especially when trying to pave my own way. This business was not my second attempt to make something happen. It was more like 14 or 15 or maybe even more. It took me entirely too long to figure out this print-on-demand thing, like two to three years of trial and error. The lesson that

I want you to learn from this is never to give up no matter what is thrown your way.

Here are some helpful tips on breaking away from your norm and escaping your 9-to-5:

- Make a clear list of goals you want to reach. Write down your weekly, monthly, quarterly, and yearly goals. Also, for the love of all things holy, *do not* write that you want to make a million dollars as a goal if you have no clear outline of how you want to get there. To make a million dollars online, you first need to make $1, then $100, then $1,000, etc. Make your expectations and goals achievable and realistic so you feel you are making progress.
- If need be—*burn your boat*. Don't do anything that will create a financial burden, but when the coast seems clear, burn the shit out of your boat and get up and grind every day to reach your goals.
- Get a mentor. This will help you stay the path and make sure you have some guidance on your journey.
- If you know you want to do something else but do not have an idea of what you want to do, think about what your passion is. What do you love to do? What can you sit and talk about all day long? Truly think about this because there is a way to make money with anything.
- *Do not give up, and do not listen to the naysayers!*

We have all experienced pain and heartache that has momentarily crippled our thought processes and will to continue to, but it is how we come out on the other side that makes us the strong and confident individuals we are today.

C.S. Lewis was right when he said, "Hardship prepares ordinary people for an extraordinary destiny."

ABOUT THE AUTHOR

Kathy L. Walls is an ecommerce and affiliate marketer who got her start on the Etsy platform with a print-on-demand business. She was able to scale her hobby into a six-figure business.

She has taken her knowledge in these fields to new heights by teaching how to make money online. Her Facebook group, Mastermind Digital Marketing Online: How To Win Online With Kathy Walls, is full of like-minded individuals looking to create an online income using platforms such as Etsy, Shopify, ClickFunnels and social media marketing.

Kathy has been married to her husband and business partner, Scott, for twenty-five years. They have two children, Trevor and Josie, and currently live in Missouri. They love boating and spend as much time as possible on the water, traveling around the U. S. and spending time with friends and family.

Find her group here:
www.facebook.com/groups/ArtOfSalesFunnels

Get your free Getting Started On Etsy course here:
www.learningetsywithkathy.com

For more information about Kathy L. Walls,
visit her site here: **www.kathylwalls.com**

THE DEMON IN MY KIDNEYS

by Carlos Gonzalez

"A joyful heart is good medicine, but a broken spirit dries up the bones."
- Book of Proverbs

I didn't understand the words that had just been spoken to me. At the same time, everything that had happened to me in the past ten years made sense. The processing of the news was what I couldn't quite grasp yet.

"Mr. Gonzalez, you have kidney failure. It's in the third stage."

The white room I was in all-of-a-sudden looked infinite. The doctor's voice seemed to be a thousand miles away. The echo in my mind, "kidney failure... failure... you're a failure..."

Suddenly it all made sense. The decade-long exhaustion. The lack of clarity. The lack of focus. The lack of motivation. The mood swings. The pain, the excruciating pain—but I had answers. Those answers validated that most of my problems were not my fault. I'm not lazy. I'm not a jerk. I'm not a failure. But my fight was only just starting, the fight for my life.

Adversity comes in many forms. For me, it turned out to be physical, mental, and emotional. When the dice rolled, I got that. Do you know what else I got? The will and determination to conquer this enemy that now had a name and face.

You see, I've never had real adversity until I was diagnosed with my illness. I was born to loving parents, and they did their best to raise me. I then did a few years in the Army, and eventually, made my way through college. I'm married and am the father of a beautiful baby girl, Adelyn Grace. What else could I ask for?

I digress. Let's go to the beginning.

I started coding websites back in the America Online-era. Back then, none of the fancy stuff existed. No MySpace, no Facebook, heck, instant messaging was still in its infancy. Ever watch the movie, *You've Got Mail?* I started two years before that movie. Yep, I'm old, but young at heart.

Out of high school, I enrolled in the U.S. Army. I had a blast. Unfortunately, I threw out my back severely when I was nineteen. My military career was over, but little did I know, I had an even more serious issue that was just waiting to introduce itself later in my life. I was not able to do the things normal teens and twenty-year-olds did, such as play sports and travel. My back was always in pain, so I dove deeper into learning to code.

College was horrible. I mean, I had great teachers that were dedicated and motivated for our success, but I enrolled back in a time where you were "guaranteed" a job once you graduated with a bachelor's degree. Any bachelor's degree. So I went in for a degree in multimedia arts and design and focused on website design. I was already good at coding and figured I could get a job somewhere and eventually retire. It did not happen that way.

About three years into my program, my career counselor called me in and said, "Carlos, your field is oversaturated. Unfortunately, the likelihood of you getting a job is less than one percent." I couldn't believe what I was hearing. That "guarantee" immediately evaporated, and I was stuck with two options. Try to look for a job anyway (which I did without success), or do what my counselor recommended when he asked, "Have you ever considered being self-employed?"

The answer was no; I did not want to be self-employed. I was already doing freelancing gigs to support myself through college, but I wanted a good 'ol paying J-O-B so I could better support my parents (my mom and dad at the time) and eventually my own family. Around this time, I was twenty-seven, profoundly overweight, and feeling the effects of the kidney failure that I didn't know I had.

After a few days of thinking about it, I set out to continue being self-employed. I still looked for a job, unsuccessfully. Before I knew it, I started making the money I would have made if employed, if not more. *Okay, there must be some merit to this self-employed thing*, I thought.

Fast forward another ten years, and that's when I found out about my kidney failure. At the time, I was depressed and ready to quit and start over. In all honesty, that diagnosis saved my career. I now had answers to my issues, and since then, I've been tackling them one-by-one.

We don't all get the blessing of figuring out why adversity hits us. If I've learned anything from this journey, it's this; you can still tackle your issues one-by-one. For me, I have to slow down because I can no longer do what a normal thirty-something-year-old can do. That's okay. Now I know. So I've reduced the number of endeavors I've been attempting (I had five businesses at one point), and it's been an eye-opening experience. I wish I would have done it sooner.

Adversity helped me learn what my limits are. As a former soldier, it was hard to accept it in the beginning, but I've conquered that now. I won't say, "If I can do it, then so can you" because we all have different demons to conquer. What I will say is that if you find yourself in any kind of adversity, you can and you will conquer that adversity if you break down the problems into smaller problems and work on them one-by-one. Notice I didn't say *solve* your problems one-by-one, because some can't be solved, only worked with. Even that, though, is solving the problem if you learn how to deal with something that can't be solved right away, and that's a win in my book.

Now, I own my own agency where I do lead generation and website design for other businesses. As of the writing of this chapter, I've hired my first set of cold callers, and I can't be more excited to be stepping outside of my comfort zone to do this. I wouldn't have been able to do this last year. My mind was not right. Now, the sky is the limit. Now, I can build something that will eventually pay for my daughter's college degree if she wants to go that route. Maybe it will pay to get her own business started. Who knows what the future holds. All I know is that it's a positive future because it's now a positive present, and I can't thank God enough for that.

ABOUT CARLOS GONZALEZ

Carlos was born in 1980 in Los Angeles, California. His mother was a homemaker, and his father was a house painter. He did what normal kids did in those days: played outside, wrestled with his friends, tormented his parents, etc. Two people in his life gave him the inspiration to have his own business: his father and grandmother. Although he admired them for it, he didn't quite feel that this was meant to be his journey. Upon graduating from high school early, he set out on another journey to serve his country in the U.S. Army and served honorably for six years in both active duty and the reserves. He started working on his undergrad degree at age twenty-four after his time in the military, wanting to get a job with his degree and eventually teach. Once completing his graduate studies, he taught at the bachelor level for two years and created a curriculum that was used for years after. He's run his own business for over fifteen years. He has a wife, Natasha, and a daughter, Adelyn. His goal is to one day sell his business and spend his remaining years enjoying his time with his family.

Find out more about Carlos on his website:
www.CarlosBuiltThis.com

Follow Carlos on Facebook:
www.facebook.com/CarlosBuiltThis

FROM LIMITED TO LIMITLESS STEP INTO YOUR POWER AND ACHIEVE YOUR FULLEST POTENTIAL

by Adri Kyser

We Fall. We Break. We Fail.
But Then
We Rise. We Heal. We Overcome.

Who do you think you are?
It didn't matter how much success I achieved in my life. Those words would continuously play in the background and affect me for years to come.

On the one hand, that question fueled my fears, self-doubts, and insecurities that being bullied and abused as a child created. On the other hand, it pushed me to do better, try harder, and achieve more.

As a child, I always wanted to make a difference in people's lives. I wanted to become a lawyer and help people who felt helpless as I once did. I learned to be strong, focused, and determined. I spent years taking more classes, going to the next training event, holding myself to higher standards, and proving to myself that I was good enough.

I mastered the skill of putting up a confident front even when I felt like I was falling apart. It was my coping mechanism of choice and my way to build a wall of protection. It took me years to realize that my vulnerability, uniqueness, and willingness to step out of my comfort zone would be one of the most significant assets in my business.

* * *

It's early morning in 2013. I have traveled all the way to China to lead a four-day training event. I find myself about to enter a room with over fifty people, all excited to be at this particular event. I have taught this training course for many years, but this is the first time I will be conducting training with the help of a translator.

I can feel my heart racing. My hands are getting cold, and the butterflies building in my stomach are telling me it's time to start. As I wait to be introduced, I get nervous. For a moment, I start to second-guess myself. Will they like me? Will they enjoy what I have to share? Will I be good enough for them?

This is familiar territory, and before I go into this rabbit hole of self-doubts and fears, I take a few deep breaths and tell myself, *You can do this. Be yourself and do your best.*

As I step into the room, I see smiling faces. As I smile back, I can feel an unspoken sense of relief in the room. I introduce myself and share that I'm nervous because my Chinese is not very good. We laugh, and I begin to teach.

During the weekend, I share more and more of my story—my struggles and victories. While only a handful of people speak English, and we come from very different cultural backgrounds, it's evident that we all share the same human needs—to love, connect, grow, and make a positive impact.

At the end of the training, we have learned, laughed, and connected at a deeper level, all because I was willing to be vulnerable and imperfectly authentic—things that just seven years before would have made me run for the hills.

* * *

We all have a persona or aspects of ourselves that we let people see. It's like being on social media but only posting the good stuff. For years, I only allowed people to see certain aspects of myself. When they looked at me, they saw a caring, passionate, confident Latin American woman who seemed to have it all together.

Those were the things I let people see, and while I'm grateful to have a loving and supportive family, thriving business, and successful career traveling the world making a difference, I did not feel I was good enough. What I didn't let people see were the emotional scars, the broken pieces, and the limiting beliefs that I had carried since childhood.

Maybe because, as women, we have been taught at an early age that we need to be perfect and handle every situation with ease and grace, from taking care of our families, our careers, and our kids, to everything between. Maybe it's because, for years, us women have had to work twice as hard to prove our worth, our value, and that we are more than our physical appearance.

Many times in my life, I had to learn to roll with the punches and keep moving forward no matter what. I had to overcome being bullied and abused as a child, as well as rise above hurtful, racists remarks about being an immigrant with an accent. I learned to hide my vulnerabilities and show only a strong front. Being strong has helped me in many areas of my life, but deep within me, I felt broken.

My aunt would ask me, "Who do you think you are, you stupid little girl?" This was followed by "You're stupid, you're fat, you're ugly." It made me feel small, unworthy, and not good enough.

The broken pieces within caused me tremendous physical and emotional pain. I suffered from chronic back pain for over a decade. What I didn't know at the time was that, in reality, I was suffering from heartache. The kicker was that as an international wellness expert, yoga teacher, and speaker with numerous certifications, I held myself to unrealistic standards. I felt that I had to be a perfect example of health, confidence, and strength at all times. I would beat myself up even more for not being good enough, healthy enough, and perfect enough, which led to intense periods of pain.

I'm sure you've experienced some form of pain in your life; pain from heartbreak, loss, failure, or even abuse. What you and I have in common is that we cope with pain the best we can with the tools we have at any given time. Maybe for you, it's eating your way through your feelings, hoping the food will ease the pain. Perhaps it's waking up at two a.m., worrying about the things that cause you stress.

For me, it meant burying all of my painful memories and emotions while building a thriving career. This type of pain, though, eventually catches up with you and affects your health, relationships, and business.

After suffering from chronic pain for over a decade and trying various conventional treatments to find temporary relief, I knew I had to go deeper. I had to address the mental and emotional aspects of myself and not just my physical pain. I didn't want a future of taking medication like it was candy just to manage my pain.

Amazingly, my journey into entrepreneurship started from the need to heal myself naturally. During the process, I learned first-hand that physical, mental, and emotional wellness is essential for optimum health, happiness, and a life full of purpose.

When your mind, body, and emotions work together in harmony, you experience health, clarity, happiness, and fulfillment. But when one of these areas is out of balance, it will affect the other two, leading to disharmony, illness, and imbalance in many areas of your life. That's why your physical, mental, and emotional health will impact the health of your business, the quality of your relationships, your finances, and more.

People often want to make more money, find their soulmate, lose extra weight, or have a successful business, yet they fail to realize that to achieve all of those things, they must do their inner work.

What many people don't realize is that what happens on the outside is a reflection of what happens on the inside. To start living to your fullest potential and have the life you always wanted, you must become aware of the thoughts, beliefs, and patterns that are constantly running in the background because they affect your emotions and behavior in positive or negative ways, both in your life and business.

As an entrepreneur or business owner, it's essential to learn how to cultivate a positive mindset, establish healthy routines, and take inspired action to grow your business. Thankfully, holistic wellness helped me heal from the inside out. I learned how to release limiting beliefs, break negative patterns, and heal from old emotional wounds. I changed my mindset, took better care of my body, and surrounded myself with people who helped me grow and get to new levels.

More importantly, for the past fifteen years, I've helped thousands of men and women improve their health, feel more confident, and grow their business by healing from past emotional hurt and releasing negative patterns. I've taught them to transform their pain into purpose and their fears into confidence.

Building my business was not always easy. I encountered multiple obstacles and difficulties. I met my share of naysayers, doubters, and people who told me I was not good enough. If you're an entrepreneur or business owner, you probably understand the roller coaster we all experience at some point in our careers or business very well. There are times when we have sleepless nights, want to quit, and second-guess ourselves.

Sometimes, it may feel like you are hitting every wall imaginable, or your business isn't growing as fast as it should. It's during those moments that having your "why" and people who genuinely believe in you and your vision is so important. Remembering your "why" will give you the strength and fuel needed to keep going, especially during difficult times. Having someone believe in you, even when you don't believe in yourself, can give you the support you need to try again.

Every time I've found myself in a situation where I wanted to quit or question it all, someone would come along to tell me about the difference I made in their lives, or how something I said or did helped them and their families.

There are three key lessons I learned from this journey I would like to share with you.

1. The quality of your physical, mental, and emotional health directly impacts the quality of your life and business.
2. Believe in yourself and know that what you do matters. There are people out there needing exactly what you have to offer.
3. Your past doesn't define you. You have the choice to turn your pains, struggles, and failures into your biggest teachers. Doing that will help you grow, evolve, and transform.

Today, when people look at me, they see a caring, passionate, confident Latin American woman who is truly authentic and willing to show her vulnerability. I may not always have the answers or have it all together, but I'm open to try, stumble, fall, and get back up again.

These six words, "Who do you think you are?" no longer haunt or hold me back. Instead, I use them to fuel my passion for making a positive impact on people's lives. Don't let what happened in your past define your health, your life, and your legacy. You get to write *your story* from this moment forward.

Picture a time where you don't have to wonder if you are worthy because you know you are worthy. Picture a time where you no longer let your doubts and fears get the most of you because you can stand fully in your power and become the person you know you are meant to be. Picture a time where you are living the life of your dreams.

Picture that time.

Now is the time to upgrade your health, mindset, and relationships.

Now is the time to step into your power and become the person you know you are meant to be.

Now is the time to start living your best life.

Now is the time!

ABOUT ADRI KYSER

Adriana Kyser is an international wellness expert who has spent the past 15 years helping highly-driven women stop feeling stressed and overwhelmed and start living a happier, healthier ,and more fulfilling life. Using her Enlightened Alchemy™ method, she has helped thousands of women worldwide achieve everything from reduced pain and stress to increased confidence and productivity. Rather than drawing from only one modality, her extensive list of certifications (including NLP, coaching, yoga, and Ayurveda) allow her to create a customized wellness experience for clients. As a brand ambassador, she has worked with Athleta and Larabar. When she's not busy hosting retreats around the globe in exotic locations like Bali, Greece, and Peru, she's being featured on iHeart Radio, Amazon Prime's *The Focus*, *Authority Magazine*, and more.

Find out more about Adri on her website: www.adrikyser.com

Get Your Free "From Limited To Limitless - Find Your Bliss Playbook" here https://soulpowerjourney.com/playbook

QUITTING = DEATH

by Todd Boczkowski

"That which does not kill us, makes us stronger."

—Friedrich Nietzsche

Someone recently approached me and asked, "How have you been able to keep such a positive attitude and outlook on life despite going through so many tragic events?"

My response was quite simple and rooted out of pure survival. "If you quit, you die." That simple philosophy has shaped my life in many ways, but especially when it comes to entrepreneurship.

By the age of just ten, my life had been turned completely upside down. It didn't start out that way. My father was an entrepreneur himself. He started an ice cream business and even dabbled in dentistry, making dentures. From my point of view, my family lived the all-American dream, and we were the all-American family. When I was five years old, my mother suddenly passed away in our bathtub.

My father, now a single parent to three kids, picked up the pieces of his life. He quickly found another woman who looked very similar to my mother. He ended up marrying her, and she even adopted my siblings and I. Nearly four years to the day after burying our mother, our stepmother passed away in our family hot tub. A week later on what would be my tenth birthday, my father was arrested and charged with murdering my stepmother.

A few weeks after getting arrested, authorities charged him with my mother's murder four years earlier. Family time went

84

from dinnertime to visits at a prison. After my father was convicted of killing both my mother and stepmother, the pain was almost too much to bear. I was around thirteen years old at the time, and the thought of suicide came into my mind. I didn't really want to die; I just wanted the pain to stop. I just wanted the whirlwind that was my life to stop spinning out of control. Mix in the typical stresses of a teenager and I just didn't know how to cope with that much loss and stress. Needless to say, I was forced into survival mode when I was just a little kid.

I would ponder why this had to happen to me. I would ask why was I dealt this hand in life. Why couldn't I just have a normal life? It would take me years to realize that surviving those tragic events made me a stronger person, and it has given me the tools for me to embrace other challenges in my life.

Entrepreneurship is not for the faint of heart. You must be willing to endure a lot of hardships. The journey is a roller coaster ride of emotions. Entrepreneurship will challenge you in ways that you wouldn't have thought possible. It seems like we're living in a time where being an entrepreneur is the "cool" thing to do. Most people will only view the success part of being an entrepreneur—they don't realize the many struggles it takes to get there.

I first started consulting for businesses when I was working as a security guard for a publicly-traded company. My work there was my third job at the time, and I was barely getting by just paying my bills. I somehow ended up getting a conference call with the corporate executives on how they could grow revenue for their business. I asked them, "You do realize you hired me as a security guard, right?" It was then that I realized that I needed to go on my own path.

Starting a business when I was already struggling was extremely tough, but at the same time, I felt like I wasn't going anywhere working three jobs already. I didn't know what I was doing at the time. I had recently gotten out of the military where I carried a gun every day for work. I never saw myself as a salesman and wasn't comfortable selling, either. When you start a business, the most essential piece is selling! There were times I ate ramen noodles for the month because I wasn't sure I could spend a lot on groceries. I watched how many networking meetings I attended because I only had so much gas money. At one point, I stretched forty dollars over two weeks. The beginning was very tough. I crawled and scratched my way to get revenue through the door for my business.

With entrepreneurship, you will have a lot of high moments along with some very low moments. As hard as it was crawling to get my consulting business up and running, I eventually gained a lot of ground. The crawling and scratching was paying off. I was getting referrals left and right, my confidence was through the roof, and I was making pretty good money on top of it.

As my entrepreneurial journey progressed, so did the challenges and adversity. There were big deals that never solidified, I lost $20,000 on Facebook ads, and there was even a separate business venture that never got off the ground. Failure is part of the success formula. That is a switch in belief systems because most of us were taught throughout our childhood that failure is a bad thing. Getting straight A's in school is a success; winning a game of sports is a success. In entrepreneurship, failing is inevitable, but the only real way to fail is to quit. Sometimes that can be easier said than done. Failure can deliver a blow to your ego, pride, and confidence.

I picked myself back up, licked my wounds, and got back to the point in my journey where I had the most success—consulting businesses with their digital marketing. That is another concept I learned with failure. Just because you failed at something doesn't mean you weren't on the right track. Maybe you didn't have the most effective execution strategy. Maybe the market conditions had changed by the time you brought your idea to market. This doesn't mean you have to start all over, either. Take what you learned from the situation and press on. Go back to the point where you had traction and start again. For me, that's helping businesses with their digital marketing needs.

No matter the adversity or failure, I continue to tell myself, "I can't quit." I think back to my tragic story. There's not a day that goes by where I don't think about it. There's a lot of adversity, some of which I'll deal with for the rest of my life. I had to come to terms with the fact that my father—my own flesh and blood, the one who helped give me life—is a cold-blooded killer. My father took the lives of two beautiful women and robbed me of many things in life that I will never get back. It's a situation that will require a lifetime of healing. At the same time, it has also given me a tremendous amount of strength in my life. If I survived a nightmare childhood like that, I could get through other life challenges, including any challenge that entrepreneurship throws at me.

Having persistence and having the will to not give up only stacks the deck in your favor to survive. My ten-year military career only reinforces that concept. The military teaches you from the very beginning to not give up. Self-defense was one of the many training courses I completed in the military. In a two-minute all-out struggle, an individual expends the same amount of energy as someone who runs five miles. You will get tired. You will want to quit. The question becomes, will you? In a life-threatening situation, if you quit, you die.

My mother and stepmother died at the hands of my father. He literally squeezed the life out of them. They fought for their lives, and unfortunately, they lost. I have used that as a catalyst for myself in many different aspects of my life, including entrepreneurship. In entrepreneurship, if you quit, your dream dies.

ABOUT TODD BOCZKOWSKI

Todd Boczkowski started his entrepreneur journey while transitioning out of the military. He was trying to figure out what he wanted to do for a career and stumbled into learning digital marketing strategies. While he was struggling working three jobs to make ends meet, Todd found himself consulting for one of his employers. This led Todd to have an epiphany, which ultimately led him to start consulting for other businesses.

Todd focuses on marketing strategy and implementation using his five-step process of having an effective sales funnel. In addition to marketing strategy, Todd also trains and consults in sales using the methodology he used to generate over seven figures in gross sales for two online brands. Whether your business needs more leads or sales, Todd can help you accomplish that. It all starts with having a digital roadmap. Connect with him to get a complimentary roadmap.

Connect with me on Facebook:
facebook.com/todd.boczkowski

TAKE THE HARD ROAD, YOU LEARN SO MUCH MORE ON THE JOURNEY

by Chantelle Paige Turner

"Every one of us is gifted with different abilities. Embrace your strengths and overcome your weaknesses. You are limitless."

—Chantelle Paige Turner

After nine months of perfect ultrasounds and doctor checkups, following all the pregnancy rules of what not to eat, taking all the vitamins, and the first grandbaby in the family, we could not have been more excited about welcoming our daughter into the word.

Water broken, we arrived at the hospital ready to endure several hours of labor before welcoming our baby girl into the world, but life often does not go as planned. As they hooked me up to the monitors in the maternity ward, there was concern because every time I had a contraction, my daughter's heart rate dropped out. Unsure of what was causing that, we were taken for an emergency C-section, and less than an hour later, our daughter was born.

Although she was considered full-term, she was very small at just five pounds and nine ounces. Other than her small size, everything seemed to be good. As first-time parents and blissfully happy to meet our new baby girl, we were moved into a maternity room where family came to welcome the newest member. Only hours into this bliss, however, our whole world began to shift.

Our daughter's temperature and blood sugar were low, so she was moved to the nursery to help her. It was there that her pediatrician saw her for the first time. He didn't know what was wrong but felt strongly that she be moved to the NICU (neonatal intensive care unit). Only twenty minutes after she was moved and connected to monitors, she had seizures that stopped her breathing.

These seizures took us down a path of three days of testing until the neurologist finally came to give us the results of her MRI. With the scans laid out on my hospital bed and family gathered into the small room, the neurologist blurted out words that will haunt me for the rest of my life.

"See this large dark area of your daughter's brain? That potion of her brain is dead."

A stroke! Somehow my infant daughter had suffered a stroke just before she was born. We were given the diagnosis of cerebral palsy (CP), and to our horror, the neurologist proceeded to physically act out how someone with CP might look as they grow up. This moment in time will be burned into my mind until the day I die.

We were lost, confused, and overwhelmed. I can honestly say I have never felt so many emotions all at the same time. I was grateful to have my daughter at all, scared for what the future would hold for her, fearful that somehow this was my fault (it happened while she was inside me), and of course, all the thoughts of "why me, why us, why my child?" ran over and over through my head.

After eleven days in the NICU, hours of meetings with social workers where they talked about all our options and the things they would help us apply for, we finally left the hospital with a mountain of paperwork, a million questions, and a lot of doctor appointments to schedule.

It took me six months to realize that nothing had been applied for as far as financial help or services, and even though my husband

and I both had good corporate jobs with great insurance, we had quickly amassed a large pile of medical bills.

I personally believe there are two types of people in this world: people who *have* problems (and excuses) and people who *solve* problems. I have always been a problem solver, so it was time to get to work. I researched services and programs for children with special needs in our state, and I applied for everything I could. I got our daughter seen by the best doctors and therapists, and a little over a year into getting services with our state, I had the conversation that would one day set me on the path to impact the world.

It's been a constant battle to get our daughter what she needs. Even with doctors prescribing things for her, getting the state to cover them is a constant war. After months of fighting to get my daughter the therapy she needed, I was on the phone with a supervisor who finally gave in to our requests as I publicly cried out of frustration. At that moment, she said to me something that took me almost two years to come to terms with, but it became the catalyst for the brand and business I now treasure today.

This woman, who had caused me so much stress and frustration for months, suggested that since I was so good at advocating for my own child, I should join their board and help fight for other children as well. I was furious! First, why should anyone have to fight this hard for their child to get what they need? Second, I had a full-time job, and my husband was gone 80% of the year for his work, so I was a single a mom most of the time; I barely had time to get what my daughter needed; how could she ever think to ask me to help others?

As things started to balance out for our own family, her words kept playing in my head. I had begun to join support networks for special needs and was starting to see that I did have value to offer. There were so many parents out there who simply didn't know of all the services available for them and their children. From that frustrating conversation years earlier, my brand, Stronger Mommy, was born.

Set on a mission to empower parents who have children with special needs and helping them get the resources, services, support, and community that they need, I went to work. I knew that as parents of children with special needs that we needed a great and supportive online community, and I wanted a place where I could share all the things I had learned so I could help others who were going through it as well.

I built a Facebook group (Stronger Mommies), set it up in a way that made sense to me, and in less than six months, I had attracted close to 3,000 special needs parents. Even more amazing, I received an invite to be a part of the Facebook Power Admins (a private, invite-only group run by Facebook). Over 90% of all my group members were (and still are as I write this) active and engaged. I felt like I really wasn't doing that much work for them, yet they were constantly telling me how much my group was helping them.

After having so many other entrepreneurs ask me how I had attracted so many group members and built up my highly engaged tribe, I reverse engineered what it was that made my group both different from others and so successful, and I began helping clients do the same thing for their businesses.

First, leverage your own adversity to connect on a very deep level with those you wish to serve. I know that my success has largely come from being very clear on who I wanted to serve and also being able to relate to them on a deep level. I get them because I was them.

Once you know the who, then it's just a matter of building an audience and finding out what to serve them.

Below are some of the simplest and most effective ways to grow and maintain a highly engaged Facebook group and why building up that asset is one of the smartest things that you can do for your brand financially.

* FIFTEEN MINUTES OR LESS PER DAY: When you set up your group the right way, you can manage it all in less than fifteen minutes a day, and engagement will happen naturally. This is simple to do, but so many fail to get it right.

Use the three questions allowed by Facebook for adding new members to a closed group to weed out who should be in your group, invite engagement, and get them on your email list.

Set up clearly defined group rules and eliminate negativity. There is enough of that in the world, you don't need it in your community

Use the poll feature inside the group to do market research and test your offers before you build them.

You only need to post two times a week consistently to maintain massive engagement. One post should allow members to share something positive that has happened in the previous week (this should tie into the pain point of your avatar). The other post should be a Live video where you either do a weekly Q&A or teach on a group-related topic. This shows your group members that you are someone who provides value, and they will want to buy your products in the future.

Engage with as many posts inside your group as you possibly can. This helps your members to love you! I prefer to use post approval so that I never miss a chance to engage on a post.

These five things might seem simple, but when done consistently, they really set you and your brand apart.

Using some of the simple but highly effective strategies that I teach, one of my clients, Jamie, was able to get started in a brand new niche, quickly build his group to over two-hundred members in just a few days, and in less than two weeks, sell eleven of them his $997 course as well as a few upsells. Jamie Atkinson went from an audience of zero to selling over $12,000, all with *zero* ad spend, by following this simple structure and leveraging his newly created Facebook group.

Most people put off starting a group or have failed with their groups in the past because they have been too focused on how they can constantly come up with engaging content to keep the members active instead of actually leveraging a strategy that grows you a highly engaged tribe on its own. By following my methods, setting up their groups the right way, and leveraging the tools I teach, my clients are able to quickly grow highly engaged groups of potential buyers, all with having no list, minimal content creation, and spending less than fifteen minutes a day on it.

To me, nothing is better in business than when you have amazing brand CULTure and tribe of engaged followers who know, like, and trust you.

ABOUT
CHANTELLE PAIGE TURNER

Chantelle Turner began her online entrepreneur journey shortly after having her daughter. She was looking for a way to help cover the medical bills related to her daughter's stroke and discovered network marketing.

While she did quite well early on using traditional methods, she quickly hit a plateau and began looking for ways to leverage the Internet and automation. During this time, she was also working hard to get her daughter the medical services and support she needed. As she found ways to help her own daughter, she realized many other parents who had kids with special needs were not getting the support they needed, either.

With her Internet and marketing skills, she founded her company; Stronger Mommy, to help other special needs parents like herself. While building Stronger Mommy, Chantelle found and developed highly effective strategies that not only grew her following and brand but revolutionized the way people grow and engaged with their tribe. Chantelle's clients who adopt these strategies have seen massive growth both in their online following and sales.

If you want more help growing your own tribe of engaged followers, head over to **www.ChantelleTurner.com/book**.

WHY REALITY IS IRRELEVANT TO ACHIEVING ANYTHING GREAT

by Lavinia Pavel

*"I felt like it was time to set up my future, so I set a goal.
My goal was independence."*

—Beyoncé Knowles-Carter

F or the past few years of my life, I have had the most beautiful experiences. I have traveled around Europe, and I visited the most beautiful beaches in Spain while working remotely for some of the biggest digital marketing influencers in America. I've been mentored, and I learned how to start, run, and grow a business from one of the highest-paid B2B coaches and consultants in America. I've been in direct contact with millionaires and billionaires. I am finally very confident about my future. I feel unstoppable because I am closer than ever to serving my purpose in the world and doing something meaningful with my life.

But how did I get here?

I have been struggling for years trying to understand the truth about this world. The elusive answer as to why some people are more successful than others and how we get to where we're going from where we've been. I started following some of the most successful people in the world and listened to them. However, with the level of understanding that I had back then,

I couldn't comprehend those messages. My reality was limited to the perspective that I was now trying to cultivate.

This is how it all started:

It was almost midnight, and I was sitting in my room, in my parents' small apartment in Romania. I was looking around, thinking about me, my life, and my past, and I felt hopeless. I was very depressed. I didn't have any close friends, and I wasn't close to my parents. I didn't have any money or resources. I couldn't see any possible way I could ever succeed in life. It was hard for me to think that I deserved anything good. I was nineteen.

After a few minutes, I opened the light again, and I grabbed Napoleon Hill's book, *Think and Grow Rich* and started reading it. At that moment, I had the biggest revelation of my life. I realized that nothing in this world could stop me from learning and becoming better. I finally discovered one thing that I have complete control upon: my mind.

For the first time in many years, I felt hope. I thought I finally found a solution to my problem and a path to achieving my dreams. I started looking for other successful people who were sharing their knowledge. I was pleased to discover that the message was similar. Over the next few months, I became obsessed with learning more and more about how we can achieve everything we want in life.

All this was great, but I was feeling such a big contrast inside. I couldn't stop noticing the reality I was living in.

In my perspective, at that moment, having financial freedom, love, and success was impossible because my circumstances could never facilitate all of that. How can a girl who grew up in a small village in Romania with no money, no connections, no financial education, and very low self-esteem ever become a millionaire? It was ridiculous even to think about it. I knew that it was possible for other people while accepting that, at least for the time being, it wasn't for me. I accepted it because I couldn't see a logical or real path that could lead me there. At that time, I was an observer. I was living my life based on the memories of the past rather than the vision of the future.

I lost hope again. I stopped reading or following anybody. I kept saying to myself, *If I lived in a different country (Romania sucks), if I had other parents, if I had more money, if I had somebody to help me*...and so on. I started blaming everything around me for my unhappiness, and I started feeling even worse than before.

One day, I read this quote by Jim Rohn: "Success is not something you pursue; it is something you attract by the person you become."

That quote was very impactful for me because I realized that making my dreams come true was not a matter of doing, it was a matter of being. I needed to change into a person who could better handle success. It was mind-blowing to realize that none of the excuses I used to have were good enough to stop me from becoming better. I was one book away, one video away, from the greatest minds in this world.

To change who I was, I needed to understand who I was. I realized that I was a sum of habits, emotions, circumstances, and beliefs. What I was living in that present moment and what I was calling "my reality" was a reflection of myself. I understood that for a fresh new start, I needed to stop the flow of my old thought patterns, so I started to meditate and calm my mind. I practiced focus, and I told myself to look for the good in every-thing constantly.

With my new level of understanding, I could see things clearer. I started replacing old thoughts and beliefs with new ones that served me better. Since I couldn't change what was around me, I changed the way of looking at things. I realized that I wasn't feeling bad because of where I was in life because that was something that I could handle. I was feeling terrible because I thought things would never change. I was using my reality to predict what was available to me or not. That was my starting point, and that's why I was only going for what I thought I could achieve and not what my dreams actually were.

I started studying psychology in college, and I started traveling more around Europe and the U.S., and great opportunities came my way. I met amazing people who helped me along the way, who offered me a job opportunity, and I was ready!

Great minds recognize each other. Winners recognize winners. All it took was somebody who believed in me more than I believed in myself. Somebody who recognized my potential and decided to offer me a chance.

I can tell you for sure that the sad, negative, and closed Lavinia could never stand a chance in front of this opportunity. We are living on the leading edge of thought and the information that is everywhere and can illuminate us and keep us from playing the victim role. Once you understand the value of being hungry, the value of the contrast for the expansion of this universe, you will feel blessed beyond description. Without our desires, there would be no curiosity, and without curiosity, there are no questions, which leads to no reception of answers and ultimately no expansion.

My advice to you is to stop, look around, accept, appreciate, and change. The reality is necessary for the creation of your desires but irrelevant for what you will achieve in the future. The only thing that will predict your future is what you are and what you are willing to become because everything is a reflection of ourselves. That's how wonderful this universe is.

ABOUT ANDREEA LAVINIA PAVEL

Lavinia is an aspiring entrepreneur and success coach who's now working directly with a multiple seven-figure earner as the right-hand person in the company. She's been behind the scenes of multiple six and seven-figure launches and actively participated in over five hundred hours of high level B2B mentoring sessions that featured millionaires and billionaires such as James Smiley, Rachel Pederson, and Kevin Harrington.

AN IMMIGRANT OVERCOMING ADVERSITY IN THE RICHEST LAND IN THE WORLD

by Sonny Tran

In the distant land of Vietnam, after a civil war of ideologies between democracy and communism that separated the north and the south of the country, I was the first-born child of an arranged marriage. After my grandmother's death, my mother, as the eldest, was left to help her father raise her seven younger siblings.

After a time, my grandfather arranged her marriage. We were poor. My father's family had money, and that was the culture in the late '70s. Because I was a boy, my mother promised herself that she would not have her son serve in the Communist Army that killed many of her relatives. She succeeded in doing this with the kindness of her distant cousin, who had a boat and helped us escape the country by sea at the tender age of eighteen months.

The seas at the time were filled with opportunistic pirates raiding, pillaging, and raping passengers on the boats—people just trying to find a better life. Food was rationed, and she did not eat because she had an infant who cried for her portion. It was five days at sea until we arrived in Indonesia, where we were refugees for five months until we were accepted to our new life in the United States of America. We then lived in Ohio for eleven months and could not find a job. An aunt moved us to Pennsylvania, where my mom's two brothers and a sister also resided.

We then proceeded to Atlantic City, New Jersey, where there was an abundance of opportunity with the rise of casino gambling. For five dollars an hour, she worked and toiled for the next twelve years; her third-grade Vietnamese education could not get her far. We did not have money and lived in the projects in the city with nine people crammed in a tiny one-bedroom apartment. One of my earliest memories was when I was four years old, sitting in a grocery store shopping cart, crying so mother would let me hold her little change bag the size of a person's palm. She gave it to me, and then a very tall man snatched it out of this little guy's hands when she looked away at the vegetables.

What could I do but cry? Mom saw the man, but her being five-foot-nothing, she was in no position to do anything, and no one stopped the man running out of the supermarket. Perhaps in the poor neighborhood, this was normal, but I just cannot forget the feeling of helplessness or the pain of me getting what I wanted. All we could do was walk home without any groceries for our family to eat for the week. I never dared ask what she did to get our family by that week, and in a sense, I feel ashamed to ask because it was my fault. God, this woman is so strong, and a great role model! From that moment on, I have been shaped to really understand sacrifice.

She saved money throughout the next few years with her five-dollar-an-hour job to purchase a house, but she always dreamed of a business so she could spend more time with her four children. So, she saved and saved, and years later, she took all of her money and cashed out her 401(k) to purchase a liquor store three thousand miles away in Colorado. We struggled to make the deal with the previous owner—an older gentleman in his late 60s, Mr. Kim. Mr. Kim owned the liquor store for many years and would only sell to the right buyer. Many people tried to buy his store and failed. My mother was able to convince him she would take care of his baby. It was so funny to observe the squabbles between two people in the super broken English accents, trying to get their points across in an argument. After a month, though, they agreed, and that's where our new adventure began.

We faced a lot of discrimination; we truly believed the competitor liquor stores had connections with the local authorities. Every year, they accused us of selling to the underaged. But my mom was brilliant and detailed at keeping records by following Mr. Kim's stubborn old ways. Through many trials, the attorney that represented us would not look at our file until the morning of the trial. But boy-oh-boy was my mother prepared with all the tapes, video, and times of alleged transactions that never truly happened. We had proof, and we triumphed.

See, even though she spoke broken English, had a third-grade education, and made no money, she did it through hard work and the sheer desire to succeed! This same liquor store allowed her to purchase her new dream home in Colorado with lots of land. This fire and inspiration trail blazed the path that led me to believe that I can do it too. So that spark and motivation that leads to my journey.

My journey starts with me being shipped to Colorado in 1997 before she pursued the liquor store to live with my rich uncle. My mother was worried about the bad influences of drugs and gangs in my hometown. Sometimes I had to walk three miles to get to school—not fun for a seventeen-year-old. Coming from the east coast and starting at a new school for my senior year of high school, I didn't have many friends. The culture is definitely different than the west coast. There were many cliques, and I did not belong.

The West was less blunt than where I grew up. They called things as they are, without the facade that everything was always great. I was able to make one friend who also was a foreigner and, like me, had moved into the area. I really studied hard and had a deep desire to make money and be like my rich uncle. My whole life, I had a brilliant cousin that everyone always compared me to. He always got straight As; I was more of a B and C student. The power of belief encouraged me to decide to take action and work hard, and that led me to what I wanted to be and do.

In high school, I became part of the National Honor Society. They had a new program called an advanced diploma, which entailed staying in high school for another year while earning college credits, all at the expense of the school system. I did that because I did not want to be a burden on my mom's new business; we could not afford out-of-state tuition. To receive the scholarship, all I had to do was maintain a high GPA with the local community college credits. In community college, I had a wonderful professor by the name of John Knowlton for micro-economics. He blew me away with how the stock market works. I got so excited from what I learned that I wanted to apply it. I saved up a little money to open a Merrill Lynch account. I got denied because they only worked with people with fifty to one hundred thousand dollars or more and said the trading fees were too high for my meager savings. They recommended a discount online broker by the name of Charles Schwab.

I was able to convince my mom to match my two thousand dollars for a total of four thousand and put it in a brokerage account, and then I started trading stocks and stock options. I was learning technical trading as well as taking on sixteen to eighteen credit hours. In about a month's time, I had forty thousand in the bank and forty thousand in stock options. I thought to purchase my mom's dream car—a Lexus—but decided to reinvest it. The stock I chose got crushed, and I was down to zero. I took my shot at the million, and it didn't work out.

After that, I was back to focusing on just my studies. With no money to invest, my last option to make money was working a side job at a deli. As any good Asian child does when you work for your parents, you don't make money. A place to sleep and hot meals are considered wages from the family business. I certainly remember that as a child. Dad, Mom, my three sisters, two uncles, and their friend lived with us in a one-bedroom apartment. That was our living situation, so when we were finally able to purchase a new home in Colorado, my own room was awesome!

I graduated high school with an advanced degree, and from community college with a 3.8 GPA. I was awarded a scholar-ship, and with my Pell Grant, was able to attend the University of Colorado for free. One day on campus, I responded to an ad by a dotcom that wanted to hire college kids to sign up other students for discounts. I thought it was great until I found out that I had to do door-to-door, prospecting businesses for the discounts. What intrigued me was a rumor they were going to be bought out by Yahoo, and that they had stock options.

They paid me a dollar for each person that signed up as a member, and a little money for every business that gave discounts to members. Joel was the trainer. A veteran at selling knives door-to-door, he helped me get over my fear of soliciting businesses, and anyone for that matter. You see, even in college, I had to take a public speaking class. I still fear public speaking to this day. It was a 1099 job, which means you owned a business. I did not fully understand that until tax time came around. Boy, was I surprised when I had to fill out that complicated form. Then, I found out the rules are pretty good for the entrepreneur.

This excitement led me to my first partnership with a person that wanted to sell cell phones, which was the in-thing in 1999. That was my side hustle while I was a full-time college student. Then I went to a seminar about being a financial advisor, where there were one hundred people seeking the same job. The competition was stiff, but I prevailed among the crop and got the job at about twenty years old. I was making money, but there was a statement made that did not sit well with me, I was told that I didn't need school—I could just make a hundred thousand dollars a year now. I thought about that for a little bit and ended up quitting the job because it did not meet my core values.

I was going to school with sixteen credit hours. I made a deal with a bank, which is now Chase, where I would work thirty-two hours a week. I told them I had the financial advisor licenses, which at the time was a series 6 and 63, and the bank could use a good financial guy like me. They were not looking but made an exception and let me go to work Monday, Wednesday, and Friday during the week, and every Saturday so I could attend school on Tuesday and Thursday. It was a good run being a banker, but I wanted to be an entrepreneur where I called my own shots. So, when I graduated, I finally quit my job and went back to New Jersey to be closer to Mommy Dearest and my sisters.

It was wonderful being back at home, and I eventually learned and acquired more skills to open up an insurance company, a mortgage company, a tax preparation business, a marketing firm, an insurance team, and a consulting company. You can do this even without speaking the language in the beginning. In kindergarten and first grade, I did not speak a word of English, but still remember making a Valentine's card with construction paper. We were so broke when I was in first grade that I didn't even have a quarter for potato chips, while all the other kids had snacks during snack time.

A few times, the poor nuns took money out of their pocket to allow me a treat once in a long while to feel like the other kids. I often stayed after school was out because no one was there to pick my sisters and me up. I just want to share these struggles with you, as I know you may have also experienced them, to let you see that you are not alone. You can achieve anything you set your mind to. This is the land of opportunity, so make it happen, and don't let money, education, or language be the barrier. Struggle is actually a blessing because it builds character and grit; it helps you appreciate and understand that you can achieve anything in this life. Take it from someone that has built his businesses with immigrants. I speak Vietnamese. My family did not speak any English when we arrived here; we needed the kind hearts of others that spoke both to help us get first jobs, and understand the framework, rules, and basics of normal American society.

That showed us the way to build the future for our family. I am so grateful for the many that helped my family and me along the way. I am paying that forward every day to people who do not understand that it is an advantage to know another language and to be able to communicate effectively. You can do business with more people than the average person. My business today helps other business owners connect the problem of sales with the online world. Processes are necessary to scale, and an automated sales processes rules, because you cannot do everything yourself and work twenty-four hours a day. Machines and processes can, though. You can duplicate yourself through the online digital world. The secret is that you are your best salesperson, and you need to duplicate yourself through automation. You can do this in your own native language to help people go through experiences and achieve what you already have. So, let's work on your strengths, achieve more, give back to society, and help others grow!

ABOUT SONNY TRAN

Sonny Tran started his entrepreneurial journey in college. He is a serial entrepreneur with six businesses. His businesses are an insurance company, a mortgage company, a tax preparation business, a marketing firm, an insurance team, and a consulting company. He has nineteen years of experience in finance and business, with a degree in finance and computer information systems. He has made six figures in his businesses and integration with them working in unison. He can help your business create a sales system that generates more revenue by taking a physical sales approach and combining that with the online world and technology.

You can get a FREE 30-day trial of his CRM at
www.yellowlabelcrm.com

Facebook link:
www.facebook.com/FinancialSonny

HOW TO OVERCOME THE INVISIBLE WALLS OF ADVERSITY TO UNLEASH YOUR PURPOSE-DRIVEN BUSINESS

by Angie Norris

Most people face a myriad of headaches, heartaches, and hang-ups. Everyone has a story, and some will make you cry, but our troubles should not define us. The way we handle our troubles is what makes us who we are.

I have strived to be the best version of myself in spite of the adversity that I have experienced in my life. To say my childhood was normal would be a lie, but the question is this: What is the definition of normal? A traumatic experience took place when I was seven years old that caused me to grow up quickly and realize that my childhood wasn't like other kids my age. The deep, dark details aren't really that important at this point, but just know that my family's life stories are beyond abnormal, to say the least.

The PG-13 version is that my parents were from two different backgrounds. My mother was born and raised in an extremely poor village in Thailand. She faced the hardest of adverse situations, and her life focused on survival. My father was born in the U.S., and upon graduating high school, he enrolled in the military to get away from his small-town roots of Illinois. While my father was stationed in Thailand at the age of nineteen, he looked across a crowded room full of people and saw my mother. He explained that, at that moment, he thought, *I just have to have her.* He walked across the room, wrapped his legs around her legs, and told her, "You are mine" and then carried her away.

My mother was only twenty-one at the time, and unbeknownst to my father, she had already been married twice and had four children. This situation was common for destitute Thai families who pushed arranged marriages onto their teenage daughters as a way to improve the quality of life for the entire family unit. That didn't seem to stop my father's determination to marry her, save her from her poverty-stricken, third-world, country life and bring her back to the United States to start his own family. My brother Bobby was born in 1975, I was born in 1977, and our first home was a tiny trailer in a very small town in Illinois. My parents didn't have much money, but for a while, life was good.

Due to the military, we moved so much that I had attended nine different schools by the time I was in high school. During that time, my parents got divorced, married, divorced, married, and later divorced. Yes, they got married three times to each other and divorced three times from each other. To say they had a love-hate for each another would be quite accurate. My father loved my mother at an almost unhealthy level, but he was extremely controlling and wanted her to be compliant, silent, and agreeable. My mother was not the stereotypical, self-servient Asian he had expected but rather a strong-willed, independent woman who had her own dreams and goals for her life, including working hard to make money to send to her four young children she had left behind in Thailand.

My father kept sole custody of us and became a single father raising two children in San Antonio, TX. Those years were extremely hard for my brother and me because we didn't fit into any of the full Caucasian or Asian communities, and we were constantly being told we were adopted due to being half Asian while our father was full Caucasian. This caused me to have major issues with my heritage, my identity, and how I interacted with friends.

Luckily, I wasn't alone because my brother was in the same position, but he faced his own demons as a result of our chaotic family life. We were latch-key kids because our father was gone all day from sunrise to sunset, so we fended for ourselves and had to be very responsible from a young age.

While my brother and I were visiting our mother for a summer when I was nine, my father remarried another woman without telling us. She was also born and raised in Thailand. Our new step-mother was the exact same height as me, and my father introduced her by stating, "This is your new mom; call her Mom," and that is exactly what we did from that day forward.

During my final year of elementary school, we moved back to that small town in Illinois where I was born. The town was 99% Caucasian, and our family stuck out like a sore thumb. During junior high, my brother and I both made some new friends, but we certainly felt that we were different and had to prove ourselves to be included by classmates, teachers, and even family members.

My high school years were emotional because I had grown a hatred for my father. The list of reasons had grown through the years, and I was counting the minutes until I graduated high school so I could get far away from him. My father set unrealistic expectations for me during high school where I was perpetually in trouble for breaking rules that my father knew I could never keep. This was his way of keeping me from enjoying childhood, sleepovers at friends' houses, fun times that high school kids got to do, and most of all, kept me in a state of fear. I was a rule-follower, straight-A student, excelled at every sport, and did my very best to always do the right thing. I never drank, never did drugs, and never got in trouble at school, but I often wondered why I was always in trouble at home. I always felt like a disappointment to my parents, and it wasn't until I was much older that I realized that my father manufactured this purposeful plan of unrealistic rules to keep me continuously grounded and under his controlling authority.

I also felt abandoned by my birth mother who had remarried, had another child, and seemed to have moved on with her life. Having never lived with her the majority of my childhood and all of my teen years left me with a yearning to get to know her and have that mother-daughter relationship I so badly wanted. Despite facing many heartaches and hurts throughout the years, I focused on excelling in school and sports.

Although my father and birth mother never went to any of my athletic or school activities, I realized that the only person I could count on was me. I knew that if I worked hard in school and sports, I could get scholarships to universities. Moreover, if I worked various jobs, I could save money to pay for expenses once I was on my own. I focused on striving for the positives in life because the negatives were always so disappointing.

The hardest part was that I felt alone, I felt different, and I was constantly wondering why my parents and upbringing weren't normal. My father told me that if I didn't live at home and attend a local university that he would disown me—and that is exactly what happened. When I was seventeen, I moved away and never returned. The number of backstories and details of my life are unaccounted for in this chapter; however, one day I hope to document these memoirs and personal accounts in a book to tell the entire story. Although much of my life wasn't rainbows and kittens, it is the story of my life, and regardless of the hurts that came with it, I'm proud of who I have become despite my upbringing. I had food, shelter, clothes, a kind step-mother, and amazing extended family support, and regardless of mistakes, I know that my parents loved me in their own way. There are people out there who have faced circumstances much worse than I ever have, and my hurt is a tiny instance on the spectrum of adversity.

Childhood stress can play a role in our adult lives, and as I grew older, I began to make many mistakes and wrong turns of my own. Striving for that sense of belonging, I married the wrong man and tried to fit into his world—a world of chaos, bad behavior, sinful activities, disingenuous people, and a marriage I certainly didn't imagine having. I found the strength and courage to divorce him regardless of embarrassment. Our life was fun, but it was not the married life that I had been dreaming of since childhood, and his actions and lifestyle were steering me down the wrong path. After my divorce, I did a lot of soul searching and chipped away any negative character traits I began to show so I could find myself. What I realized is that I had to really figure out who I was, embrace my hurts and past, be vulnerable and transparent, and surround myself with people who accepted me for who I am, baggage and all, and not for who they wanted me to be.

I was pretending to be someone I thought everyone wanted me to be, and I pushed down the hurts of my past to a subterranean level of my soul where no one would ever know about my pain. Unfortunately, by not facing my demons, there were consequences. I wasn't at peace with who I was or where I came from. I had a battle of loving my parents for the goodness in them, but I couldn't let go of the hang-ups they caused me as a result of their choices. I had to face the fact that I had an invisible wall of adversity that I thought if I suppressed, would be out of sight and out of mind. Nothing could have been further from the truth. Until I faced my pain, I was paralyzed and couldn't move forward.

I had this inner voice telling me that I was meant for more, but I was held back by the aftermath of being a casualty of my childhood circumstances. No one was to blame but myself for standing in my own way on my own path to greatness. Once I figured out how to get past my pain, I was able to fuel my energy toward being the best version of myself in all aspects of my life, both personally and professionally. I had to work to overcome my past hurts that kept me from my true potential. Without that work, I would not have opened my guarded heart to the people I have in my life today, and I most certainly would not have had the courage to start my own business.

Since the age of thirty, I have finally felt a sense of belonging with friends, loved ones, my new husband, and now extended family. My whole life, I tried hard to fit in when I should have been focusing on trying to stand out. I had finally embraced my past, become proud of my heritage, and was happy about the person I had become. I made the decision to forgive, focus on positives, and cherish the moments with my parents while I had them in my life. As an adult, I got to know my birth mother at a much deeper level, as well as allowed my father to spend time with me, my husband, and my three children before he passed away. Although it wasn't always easy, I'm thankful I chose this path to rise above the walls of adversity, embrace where I came from, and understand that my parents faced their own set of adverse tribulations throughout their lives. Understanding their challenges and heartaches allowed me to appreciate and love them.

Adversity comes in various forms, and no matter who you are, you have probably faced adverse situations in your life. Some of you have had difficult and unforgettable situations, while others have experienced mild doses. Whether you had physical, mental, emotional, social, spiritual, financial, or entrepreneurial adversity, you had to take steps to overcome your adversity to move forward. I don't tell the story of my background of adversity because I want sympathy but to show people that although adversity can place bricks of sadness, fear, resentment, or hurt around your heart, there is still the option of chipping away those bricks in order to heal and move toward happiness.

How did I unlock my true potential? How did I move past the pain and towards pleasure? How did I realize that, although I was a victim, I was using it as a crutch to stay in the safe zone of being untouchable? For me, I took several steps to help become the best version of myself. Depending on your hurts, hang-ups, and heartaches, you can alter these tactics to aid you in your journey of self-transformation to overcome the invisible walls of adversity.

Be honest with your past. By embracing your past self and circumstances, you are able to shift your focus away from the chapters where adversity and pain exist and open new chapters focused on happiness.

Strive for self-awareness. By having clarity of your personality, character, feelings, motives, desires, emotions, beliefs, and weaknesses, you can tackle the traits that are holding you back and focus on the ones that can carry you forward.

Own the impact of invisible wounds. Loss, shame, guilt, fear, anxiety, grief, hurt, embarrassment, resentment, and confusion are shared by so many who experience adversity. Understand which of these feelings are keeping you from moving forward by learning how to cope with each of these pain points to overcome them.

Focus on healing and transformation. If you want to be happy in life, focus on the healing process of working through your pain so you can transform into the person you really want to be and toward a place of contentment.

Find an outlet for therapy. Every person deals with pain in various ways. By finding your favorite outlets, you can begin the therapy you need to move past the pain.

Choose faith over fear. When you live in a state of fear, you build walls around yourself and hinder yourself from experiencing happy moments and meeting genuine people. By focusing on faith, your desire to overcome adversity becomes greater than your fear.

Understand that you are not alone. The reality is that there are many people who face adversity similar to you. In fact, you may realize that there are many people who experienced harder and harsher traumatic circumstances in their lives. By coming together, you can gain empathy, wisdom, support, and healing.

See the strengths in adversity. Look for the learning opportunities in every adverse situation. As much as you want life to be a smooth ride, you grow in your faith, resilience, and coping mechanisms with each struggle.

Emulate adversity warriors. All around you are people who have faced grave adverse situations and came out the other side stronger and even more inspiring.

Avoid toxic relationships. Nothing keeps you remembering times of hurt and heartache than people who are constant reminders. Stay away from those who purposely try to bring out the worst in you or possess toxic behaviors.

Let go of self-defeating and unproductive thoughts. Often, you can become paralyzed by the mindset your past has given you. Understand that this is only keeping you from moving forward and producing results.

Realize that suffering is optional. Pain, heartache, and memories are part of life, however suffering indefinitely is a choice you can control.

Harness the power of forgiveness. The hardest of these tactics is forgiveness, yet it has the most powerful impact on you. The effort to forgive those who have hurt you can untrap you from the web of hatred and resentment.

Redirect toward your true potential. Let each success energize you toward your true potential. Small wins daily, no matter how personal or professional in nature, can propel you toward bigger wins.

Stop playing the victim. There are no benefits to playing the victim to your circumstances and situations. No matter who was at fault, rise above the victim mentality.

Stay positive, always. The power of positivity is truly remarkable. Moods are contagious, and the more positive you are, the more your surrounding people will be, too.

Harness the power of new beginnings. Despite the circumstances you have faced, you have an opportunity to provide a happier life than you experienced for those around you.

Seek clarity on your purpose. Figuring out your purpose in life can be one of the most effective ways to get you started on the path to happiness. When you can determine your purpose, you leverage your talents, skills, abilities, and gifts to influence others.

Find a competitive advantage. Extreme adversity fosters creativity and innovation, both personally and professionally. When you experience a problem, it becomes an opportunity to discover or build ways to thrive in advantageous ways.

Provide purposeful impact. When you choose to focus on others, your purpose becomes greater than you. You are then able to create lasting and meaningful opportunities for your community.

Rise stronger through entrepreneurship. Hardships can build mental strength, which proves that you are stronger than your circumstances. Couple this with your entrepreneurial spirit and talents, and you can rise to astounding achievements and accomplishments.

Unleash your purpose-driven business. The emotional strength and resilience you've developed through your adverse situations can help you build a business with a culture that stands for respect, understanding, compassion, and acceptance.

There you have it, a long list of tactics that could potentially help you begin to think differently about the hurts, hang-ups, and heartaches that were results of your adversity. Whether we like it or not, adversity is a part of life. However, overcoming adversity can be the biggest hurdles we face. How we deal with struggles, challenges, and difficulties builds character, courage, resilience, and strength. Don't let adversity keep you from pursuing your dreams. For years, I allowed the hurts of my past and insecurities from adversity keep me from becoming the entrepreneur that I wanted to be. If you overcome the invisible walls of adversity, you can unleash your purpose-driven business to finally be part of something greater than your circumstances.

ABOUT THE AUTHOR

 Angie Norris, the founder of TVpreneurs Entertainment Network, is an advanced online marketer who specializes in building, launching, and managing TV channels as apps on Roku, Amazon Fire TV, Apple TV, and other streaming TV platforms to help individuals and businesses get their messages heard by millions of people around the world, tap into a multi-billion dollar market, add new income streams to their business portfolios, and get ahead of their competition through the power of TV.

Angie has worked in marketing for over twenty years, primarily in information technology, working for Fortune 500 companies. Her skillset includes video, graphics, web and sales funnel design, as well as TV channel and mobile app development. She prides herself on learning new and often difficult emerging technologies as well as training others to leverage cutting-edge tools and resources.

Be sure to access your free TV channel masterclass at
www.tvpreneurs.com/masterclass

HAPPINESS LEARNED, LOST, THEN LEARNED AGAIN THROUGH ENTREPRENEURIAL ADVERSITY

by Aaron Stewart

I ignored the first two "emergency" texts. They were from clients who always complained, and it was Christmas Eve, for crying out loud. Surely, they could wait a few days. However, when I got the third text, I knew we had a problem because this client only contacted me after his efforts to correct something had failed.

So, I went to my computer to log in and run some quick diagnostic tests on our servers. I couldn't log in; the servers weren't responding. It was weird. I called our facility's 24/7 hotline only to find that all their systems were up, running, and showing "all green." A feeling of dread started to build in my gut when I learned it wasn't a facility problem. I knew what I had to do. At around 6:00 p.m. on Christmas Eve, I hugged my wife and my young children and left to drive across town to manually check on our servers.

As I entered the server room, I shivered. Those rooms are always so cold! I scanned the space. I could see stacks of other servers, all with their lights blinking and their hard drives humming, performing exactly as they should. However, our space stuck out. It was dark. There were no lights blinking happily; it was sadly silent with no hard drives humming. I walked over, pulled out the keyboard, and tried everything I knew to do to start them up, but nothing worked.

I called our server guy, who wasn't thrilled to hear from me on Christmas Eve. He was on call, though, so he had to pick up. We tried everything he knew how to do. Nothing we tried would bring the servers back to life, so he told me he was on his way.

We had been super conservative when we initially set the servers up. We engineered them to be triple-redundant, with a full back-up every hour. We didn't want to leave anything to chance. We wanted to make sure we would be up 100% of the time and prevent losing even a single line of code or a second of client work. So how was it all dead now? How did all three systems fail?

We lost everything—all of our coding, transaction history, customer data, and months of back-ups. All of it was on a variety of drives that were now seized up and useless. Even after spending thousands of dollars on a hard drive disaster expert, he wasn't able to retrieve anything usable. We were out of business just a few months after achieving our goal of 1,000 monthly paying clients before the end of the year. Moreover, I had also missed Christmas Eve and eventually Christmas Day with my cute family.

However, at that moment, staring at a stack of useless servers, I was struck by something profound. I realized that even with all this extra lousy stuff going on, I wasn't any more miserable than I had been for quite some time. Thinking on it, I realized that since we had reached our 1,000-customer goal, my mood, zest for life, and our little company had taken a massive nosedive. I was utterly miserable. I sat down on the cement floor in total disbelief. I put my head in my hands as my mind raced.

I felt no hope, and it had nothing to do with the servers. I had stopped making goals. There was very little was that important to me anymore, and none of it added up. I had done everything I'd learned from teachers, counselors, professors, gurus, friends, and family that would guarantee success and happiness. Yet, there I was. The success, notoriety, and wealth had come as promised, but the happiness and satisfaction were absent.

I had gone to college, completed advanced degrees, worked in corporate America to gain experience, married very well, had three terrific, healthy, and bright children, started a few businesses, worked hard to become successful, and yet I sat there alone with my misery level so high that, strangely, the disaster of our dead servers didn't seem to add to it.

Over the next few days, my disbelief developed into frustration. Eventually, that frustration turned into anger. Why was I not thrilled, content, and happy with what I had accomplished? Why did it take a server crash for me to realize that I wasn't happy?

My anger eventually motivated me to find a solution to my unique (or so I thought) challenges. One thing was clear, I now knew that happiness and peace of mind did not come from achievement. It didn't much matter if these achievements were related to academic, business, or personal growth; none of them provided the benefits I thought they would or should. For me, achieving goals of any kind had turned out to be just checkmarks on a long-term to-do list.

I knew I had to unravel this mystery. I started seriously researching, poring through the latest papers and data. I felt motivated. I didn't want to start rebuilding our business, work to make it successful, and find out yet again that success didn't equal happiness. It felt terrific to be taking action to find answers for a better life.

Interestingly, I found research that showed that goals weren't all that effective in increasing achievement. Research shows that 92% of all goals die incomplete. That was hard to comprehend at first. If goals were so bad at getting results, why were so many of the "experts" telling us that setting goals was the path to living our dreams? Things started to click for me; it was a paradigm shift. This data was the first bit of evidence to suggest that what I had believed all along was not accurate—that achieving goals did not automatically deliver the happiness so many frequently promised.

During this period, we rebuilt our business. We started from scratch, but this time around, I was determined to find joy in the daily activities of life and work. I was not going to wait to reach some future target before I celebrated. I plowed through self-help books, listened to some great books on tape, and purchased a few personal growth courses. However, my answer to the best way to live consistently happy came to me unexpectedly from a vivid memory.

I had taken our eleven-month-old daughter downstairs so she could play and practice walking on carpet instead of the hardwood floors we had upstairs. When I put her on the floor, she went to work. She stood herself up, walked a few steps, fell, then did it all over again. My wife and I were there, clapping, smiling, and encouraging her every effort. At the same time, our son came and showed me a Lego creation he'd just finished. It was a spaceship. He loved to build spaceships. I know it took him quite a bit of time and effort to put that galactic cruiser together, but my comment to him was something like, "Cool bud, now go and make sure you pick up the Legos off the floor so your sister doesn't get hurt."

His little face was hurt. My response wasn't what he wanted, and he slowly walked back to his workbench. Frustrated, he threw his spaceship into the Lego bin with a loud crash. He got my attention. At first, I thought to myself *drama*, but then it hit me.

There was our daughter standing, falling, getting up again, receiving praise for each little effort, and there was our son, crestfallen, frustrated, and now slowly cleaning up his toys after receiving far less approval than he wanted. He had been listening to us encourage his sister for her efforts but had not received any for his. He had kept building, hoping that when he finished, I would be impressed and praise him. I did neither. And again, there I was not praising him for his efforts to clean up, while I continued to heap praise on his little sister just for trying. How cruel!

Our boy was sad, disappointed, and confused. He too had once received praise for his every effort. Now, life had switched on him. The rules had changed, and it wasn't his fault. He found himself living in a world without praise for effort, and he was struggling to find happiness as he had before.

It's the same for most of us. From a very early age, we received praise for our efforts, both great and small. There was nothing to fear then. We were safe, happy, and mostly carefree. However, as we got older, recognition for our efforts was unceremoniously withheld, and we received praise only for our completed tasks. If we cleaned our rooms, got good grades, won a game, or finished our chores, there was a chance someone might notice and provide a few kind words. It was better than nothing, but not as fulfilling as it once was. We adjusted, grew up, and eventually moved on, entering the real world, where it got worse.

On our own, no one seems to notice our efforts. Even our achievements do not receive the praise we feel they should. Rather than viewing the world as messed up, we instead start to believe that we need to achieve bigger and better things to earn the recognition we seek. We worked hard to feel safe and happy again, and we hoped the new world might be the place to find it. It isn't.

My research and memories made all of this clear to me. The world doesn't reward us for effort, and it never will. The only choice we have is to adjust our mindset, change our expectations, and implement new self-sufficient strategies.

This revelation happened for me thirteen years ago, and today I am pleased to report I have never been happier or more at peace. I've proven to myself and others that living a comfortable, productive, impactful life has little to do with success, money, notoriety, or achieving any specific goal. It has little to do with our occupations, degrees, the cars we drive, or the countries we have visited. In fact, it is quite the contrary.

Lasting happiness is found in how we choose to live our lives daily, and it is very much a choice. We all need to get back to living and learning the way we did in our younger years. Yes, it is different now. We are adults with more responsibilities, experiences, opportunities, and challenges, but the patterns that worked so well in the past are the same ones that will work now. It's only the players who have changed.

Making this adjustment has been a wonderfully rewarding experience. Happiness, peace, and optimism are the new standard in my life. The company we were rebuilding back then did well. Eventually, it grew up to over 200,000 paying clients. Moreover, what made this achievement most exciting was that this time around, the result for me was precisely the opposite it had been. In that server room all those years ago, I had no more room to be more miserable. This time around, I felt I had no more room to be any happier. The success didn't add to my happiness, and that is a far better way to live.

Earlier, I knocked on goals a bit. In my research, though, I learned that goals are not the problem after all. It was the purpose of goals that I didn't understand. Goals can be fantastic if viewed appropriately. Goals should help us find direction, provide milestones, and reassure us that we are moving in the right direction. However, accomplishing a goal never delivers anything more than a checkmark on a list. Goals are not a destination, they are merely a mile marker on a never-ending path of improvement.

As an example, our daughter did not find her happiness *after* she had learned to walk, talk, or read. The encouragement and praise she received during the process provided her the happiness she needed during those difficult learning periods. She didn't wait for the outcome. And how successful is this method in learning hard things? How many people do you know who still choose to crawl? Also, if you happen to talk to someone who has lost their ability to walk and had to remaster this skill, they will tell you how difficult it really is.

This effort-focused strategy also makes failure nothing more than a milestone. For example, when we make an effort, are then rewarded, but do not achieve the desired outcome, it doesn't matter much. We have already received encouragement each step of the process. The failure itself is an afterthought and has little to no sting. We have already learned how to be happy for our effort and not to wait for happiness.

Now that we know there is a better method, and that we are experienced in living and growing through this method, you may be wondering how you can restart this currently dormant personal progress power cell?

First, we need to learn to notice and celebrate each time we put forth an effort. It sounds simple, but it turns out to be tricky. We also must take responsibility for our praise and encouragement. We need to accept that the support will not come from an outside source, and we need to stop hoping it will. That ship has long since left the harbor.

So, my challenge today is to have you commit to getting back to how you used to learn—to take responsibility for your encouragement to create the lasting peace and happiness you deserve in your life. Here are a few steps to get you started:

1. Tomorrow morning, make a list of all of the activities you will participate in that day. The list might include working on a project, yard work, a workout, a lunch appointment, whatever. Then, write them all down.

2. Throughout the day, when you make any effort, mark it down next to the activity it is most associated with, and say to yourself, *nice job* or *good work* or whatever feels right. This simple action is the gateway to tapping back into the effort wiring we used as children. It is most effective if the compliment is associated with an effort and not to any finished task or an outcome. We must make this distinction. We reward the action itself, not the completion of a task. We start to again see accomplishments as a natural consequence of taking action. As an example, efforts could include starting your car (appointment), putting on gym shorts (workout), or listening to a voicemail (work). Start by noticing each effort and reward yourself for the action.

3. Continue this process for a few days and document changes you notice in yourself. Once you reignite this original system of rewarding effort, you will feel less fear, less stress, calmer, and more peaceful. It's such a fantastic experience to once again benefit from the effort, just as we did all those years ago.

The next step is to introduce goals into this system, which will help us accomplish more than we ever have as well as accomplish them with more energy and motivation, but that is a lesson for another day.

Remember, you already have this system in place—you always have! Now, let's awaken it and get back to living, learning, and growing more organically and healthily.

ABOUT AARON STEWART

Dr. Aaron R. Stewart, MBA, Ph.D., has earned a B.S. in Economics, an MBA in International Management, and a Ph.D. in Organization and Management. His dissertation research focused on the perception of entrepreneurial opportunities in citizens' home countries and was successfully conducted in over thirty countries.

After graduation, Aaron spent a few years in corporate America to gain experience, then launched his own consulting and technology companies. He has founded or co-founded over a dozen start-up companies, including AcuTrans, Earth's Foods, SoloSEO, Utah Global Investments, and Sync Box. His clients have included a number of Fortune 100 companies. Aaron has continued his entrepreneurial research and has lived the life of entrepreneurship for the last thirty years, visiting over fifty countries in his work.

He is happily married to his wife, Carol. They have three "almost perfect" children together.

Dr. Aaron R. Stewart can be contacted at
www.draaronstewart.com

BELIEVE IN YOURSELF, TRUST YOUR GUT, TAKE ACTION

by Sheree Wertz

"If you believe you can or you believe you can't, you're right!"

—Henry Ford

You have an idea, a vision, a dream that you know in your heart will be successful. You know with every fiber of your being that you were meant to do something that would make the lives of others better. It is a dream that you've had since you were very young, and you just can't let it go until you make it happen. There are so many reasons why you put your ideas and dreams on a shelf. Those reasons are your life's journey. I have learned so much about myself in the last year, and I hope to inspire you to turn your vision and your dream into a reality.

I was raised in a household where we heard, "You can do whatever you set your mind to." My story is more about determination, perseverance, learning the hard way, trusting yourself, and yes, a little stubbornness. Most importantly, it's about believing in yourself, not giving up, trusting your own instincts, and finding the right people to guide and help you.

Like everyone, I had an eventful childhood that created the fabric of my life. My eyesight has always been poor; I got my first pair of glasses when I was seven. Before I got glasses, I didn't know there were signs or that the trees had tops and birds flew over them. Talk about an eye-opening experience!

As a very young child, I was diagnosed with anemia and had frequent high fevers. Treatment at the time was liquid iron for the anemia and tetracycline for the fever. What wasn't known then was that both medications stain the permanent teeth while they are developing so they erupt discolored and stained. My permanent teeth were gray in color with deep orange stains on my two front teeth. This resulted in being bullied throughout my grade school years. While it was a confidence-breaking time in my life, it also became the reason that I wanted to help others.

At nine, I was shot in the temple by a neighbor who was also nine. He was carrying a pump Winchester BB gun around the neighborhood. He aimed it at me and pulled the trigger. He didn't mean to hurt me; he was a kid too. The wound required surgical intervention. It was a traumatic incident that compounded my vision and learning issues. That same year, I was tripped on the icy playground, fell, and broke my arm.

At twelve, I had to have surgery to move the ulnar nerve that had become stuck between my growing bones. I rode a bus and became a captive audience of one boy who made it his mission to call attention to my discolored teeth and my surgically-bandaged arm, encouraging others to join in his taunts. I felt like a total freak and became more insecure and withdrawn.

I also struggled to learn and express myself. Schoolwork was a challenge. I had to work and study harder than my classmates just to keep up. Many times, I thought I was just not smart enough. I didn't see the things the way others did. It wasn't until I was in college that I realized there was a name for my struggle—dyslexia. Knowledge and tools have helped to ease the struggle.

During high school, I attended a vocational school and trained as a dental assistant. A highlight was winning a dental terminology contest, which provided me the opportunity to be part of a regional competition. This was a huge triumph for me. For the first time in my life, I felt like I was good at something. It also laid the groundwork for what was to become my career.

I got my degree as a dental hygienist and met my future husband who was studying to become a dentist. We were married and started creating our life together. I hadn't given up on my dream; I just put it on hold to build our dental practice.

We had difficulty conceiving a child. I had eight miscarriages and was told by several doctors that I would never carry a baby to term. We went through two rounds of in vitro fertilization, also ending in miscarriage. We were devastated. I wish I had the words to explain how I felt each time I was told I would never carry a child to term. I do, however, have the words to tell you I never believed it to be true. I never believed any of those doctors; I *knew* I would have a child. Each time, I simply said, "You aren't the right person to help me, so I'm moving on until I find that person."

I did find the right doctor. The first day I saw him he gave me the one thing I needed most—hope. He heard my story and asked me to give him three months. He was sure we could deliver a baby to term. In three months, true to his word, I was pregnant and carried a baby to term. My husband and I were ecstatic, and we were blessed with a healthy baby girl. Today, she is a very beautiful and confident young woman.

With the miscarriages behind us and a new baby daughter, we were given an opportunity to adopt a child. We weren't looking for another child; however, the mother believed we would give her child a loving home. We happily accepted and settled into being the happiest we had ever been. Until an adoption is final, the birth mother has a right to change her mind, and this one did. She sent us an email and told us she would be coming to get the baby—the very next day. There was no warning, no phone call—only an email. The loss of a child, even if you didn't give birth to that child, is disappointing and devastating. We went from the highest of highs to the lowest of lows. It's not something I want to re-live.

Within those two months, we would lose a nephew to suicide. We lost several other close family members in a short time after that. I know loss is a part of life's journey, but all of these losses took their toll.

I have always lived my life in the present; I don't worry about what might happen. We had been through some traumatic experiences, and together, we adjusted and worked through it. Or so I thought.

One day, my husband came home and told me he didn't need or want me in the office anymore. The receptionist had packed up all my things. He brought them home, handed them to me, and made it very clear that there was no need for me to go back to the office. *What?* What was happening? Where was this coming from?

Together, we had built a six-figure dental practice that was successful and thriving. Although not perfect, our life was good. I thought we were on track and that we would do great things together. In an instant, my life as I knew it changed. I would lose my job, my house, and my family. I was in total shock. For the third time, my life had been affected by someone else making decisions over something I had no control over.

It took me a while to figure out what was going on. When I did, I just moved on and didn't look back. It was the most demoralizing experienced in my life, yet it was also the best thing that could have happened to me.

As I began to evaluate my life, I realized I had never been supported by the one person who was supposed to support me. Every time I had an idea or expressed my desire to see my vision come to fruition, I was told it wasn't a good idea and that I needed to be happy with what I had. The support just wasn't there, and now I knew why.

During those twenty-five years, I believed all the things that were said to me: that my ideas wouldn't work, that someone had already done that, that my ideas didn't have value, and that I just needed to be happy and not look for more. For a time, I let those comments change who I was. Now, I was free to be me.

They say when one door closes, another opens. My mind was opened to possibilities. I put on my big-girl pants and became determined to ensure that no one was ever going to control my life again. I started moving forward and taking action. This is where my real story begins.

When I took a personal inventory, it became apparent that I have a great support team in my family and friends. I have the type of career that would allow me to support myself and my daughter easily, and I never lost sight of my vision or dream. I was still me—the hard worker, the optimist, and the person with more ideas that I knew how to implement. Speaking of those ideas, not only had they been good ideas; they were great ideas that had been turned into thriving businesses by someone else. Oddly, this gave me confidence. It was confirmation that I did, in fact, have good, viable ideas.

When things happen in life, you have choices. You can choose to go down the rabbit hole, or like the Phoenix, you can rise from the ashes. The decision is yours and yours alone. I know this may sound melodramatic, but it's the reason I shared the details of my story. It's what I feel I have done. Like the Phoenix, I have risen above all that has happened. I am a new and better version of myself. Give a girl some latitude!

I've been so busy telling my story that I forgot to share my vision. I have worked in many varied dental settings through-out my career. My training and skill set allows me to work an accelerated schedule so I can see more patients in a day. I love to educate patients and share my passion for good oral health. The connection between oral and systemic health was apparent to me long before it became mainstream. With my experience, I know how to create an educational training environment for the private sector that will engage the dental profession to take action and change their way of thinking. Many of my patients have told me that no one has given them the information that I have. Dentists have said, "How do I clone you?" Hygienists have asked my secret about how to find jobs and work an accelerated schedule. I have received a lot of feedback from my target market. I know the interest and the market for what I am offering exists.

I had written all the educational material. The issue was that I had so many ideas that I didn't know how to focus and make them into a viable business. This has been a huge struggle for me. I had so much to give, and I knew the audience was there. I wanted to do it all. I wanted to have multiple sources of income, so if one went away, I wouldn't lose everything. Again.

One of my problems was that I didn't know what I didn't know. Sometimes that is still true. Learn the questions you need to ask. That may seem obvious, but it's not. If you don't know what you don't know, you can't ask the right questions or find the right people to help you.

Another problem is my lack of technical knowledge and skills, especially regarding digital and social media. In fact, it's probably my greatest obstacle. My old way of making training videos had become obsolete, and finding the right people to help me has been a real challenge.

I have received a lot of advice, wasted some time, spent money that I didn't need to spend, and spent money I didn't have, but it was all a learning experience. It's brought me to where I am today. Most importantly, I am moving forward.

It's been a long road, and it was the journey I needed to take. I have my way of doing things, and they don't always sync with the norm. It's also what makes me unique.

When there is a need, I believe people present a solution; the key is to recognize the opportunity and use it. There are all levels of encounters. Some offer advice, some give you guided direction, some offer to do the work for you, some charge a fee, and most importantly, some mentor you. They are all a gift to you, and you should use all of them. They will give you good and bad information. It's all useful, even if only to show you what you shouldn't do. You have to take action.

The one thing that has become apparent to me is that I have to do things the way that works for me. Every time I didn't listen to my gut instinct, I have ended up regretting it, even when my actions go against all the mentoring advice. That doesn't mean that I don't respect the advice given to me by my mentors; it means I have to trust my judgment. Do you a see a theme here?

One word of caution—do your research. I am quick to jump all in. Many will say they can help you, and *they* believe they can. Do what you can to make sure they are selling what you need. I needed the basics. I was a babe in the woods. I needed detail, and most are not selling detail. They assume you know technology, and consequently, they assume a lot.

That's another point for you. When you are developing your product, you need to know your target market and the level of detail they require. Know how they learn. It will allow you to hit the ground running because you have met a need from the get-go. You will still learn and define your product, but you will be ahead of the curve.

I want to talk about the mentors that have brought me to where I am today and give them the recognition they deserve. They are crucial to my success, and I appreciate everyone one of them. There have been many from all walks of life, including family and friends. Those that have advanced my trajectory are Russell Brunson, Steve Larsen, Marley Baird, Kolton Krottinger, and James Smiley. I don't have enough time or word space to give you the details; maybe in another book. Just know that I didn't do it alone.

To sum up my advice to you:

Mindset: Keep a good mindset. It's the difference between success and failure. Know the difference between adversity and opportunity. Always see adversity as an opportunity.

Strengths: Know your strengths. Yes, you do have them. Believe in yourself and use what you already have!

Limitations: Know your limitations and find people to help you.

Ideas: Put your ideas on paper. You have to write it down to clarify in your mind what you are trying to solve and, hence, sell. You will be able to edit your thoughts easily and look back to know how far you have come.

Focus: This is a big one. Did I mention that I have a lot of ideas? Yeah, well, you can't do them all, at least not all at once. Your focus will change several times in the beginning. You have to narrow your ideas down and focus. Learn to focus early in the game. It will save you time.

Take Action: When you take action, things will fall into place. You have to take action to see any results.

Don't Compare: Do not compare yourself to anyone else. We all go at our own pace, and we all want different things—car, house, financial freedom, time with your family. So, don't compare. Know what you want and make it happen.

Be Grateful and Patient: Be grateful for what you have and all of those who have helped you. Be patient for what is to come. Success and failure are both good things.

We are all in this together. We will succeed. Only you can make it happen!

ABOUT SHEREE WERTZ

My name is Sheree Wertz, and I am a registered dental hygienist, educator/trainer, author, and entrepreneur. I have worked in the dental field for over thirty years and still have a passion for dentistry.

As a child, I had health issues and an unfortunate set of circumstances that led me to have poor oral health and poor self-esteem. Getting my teeth fixed changed my mindset and the way I felt about myself.

Cavities are the number one preventable childhood disease. I believe we can reduce that number through education.

I am bringing awareness to how your oral health is connected to your overall health.

Is your lack of oral hygiene making you sick?

Do you brush twice a day?

Do you have any oral health concerns?

I have an education series to help establish a good oral health routine.

If you would like more information, go to
dentalhygiene411.com

THE POSITIVE MINDSET OF A SINGLE MUM
The Solopreneur Journey

by Toni Barnett

"Don't wish it were easier, wish you were better."

—Jim Rohn

One thousand, two thousand, three thousand, four thousand, five thousand, Geronimo!

Yes, I did it. I jumped out of a perfectly good airplane, and it didn't end well. There was definitely some adversity to overcome. Over many years and operations to repair the damage, there would be a ton more misadventure stories to tell going forward. This, however, is a standout because it marked the beginning of my entrepreneur journey that would change my life forever.

Prior to that epic event, I was a happy mum of two awesome kids. We had a great life. I was as heavily involved in my sports as they were. I was a member of an elite squad of women rowers who had their sights set on the national team and beyond. I was also working full-time as a physical education teacher. What could be better?

There have been way too many "overcoming the odds" scenarios of wins and losses to tell here, but I would like to share with you some of the gold nuggets I discovered along the way. They have served me well through my three-decade-long entrepreneurial journey.

I am a proud and patriotic seventh-generation Australian. I'm a high school drop-out and was pregnant and married at sixteen—in that order. I was a teenage mum at seventeen. My dad passed away from cancer at age forty-two, and I divorced my husband after four years at age twenty-one. Life goes on as a single mum of two. We relocated to a state housing estate on the wrong side of town. I graduated from teachers college and got a job as a physical education and classroom teacher. Yay! I was in "the system." Upon reflection, I'm not sure if that was a good thing.

Not long after that skydiving incident, as it is affectionately referred to by my family, I established my first business—Corporate Focus, Sports Marketing. I was twenty-nine. I was the principal and CEO of that business for just over seven years. During that time, my younger brother fell victim to the AIDS epidemic and lost his battle at age thirty. I lived and worked in South Africa for two years as a consultant and the CEO of a start-up.

I returned to Oz to deal with the fallout of a major episode of post-traumatic stress. I recovered slowly, met my future husband, and we started up his real estate and business brokerage. I went back to my teaching roots and retrained as a certified life and business coach and NLP practitioner, and subsequently launched Strategic Pearls Coaching. The fallout from the global financial crisis hit us hard, our businesses suffered, and the stress was out of control. My husband, Neil, had a heart attack as a result.

We lost everything and were homeless for over a year. We started again and bought a hospitality business in Perth. We worked over one-hundred hours a week at what would become known as the worst time in the history of the Australian market to buy. We put the hospitality business into administration two years later, but this time, we knew more. We had reference to past mistakes, so we managed to regroup much quicker than previously. It was still tough. During this time, my mum became ill. I removed life support as she lost her battle in the same year.

And here I am, three years on, and have reinvented myself, my life, and my business online.

I see that the adverse situations that we find ourselves in are simply life events—it's the lessons we take from them and how we deal with them that matters. I don't mean to downplay those tragic or traumatic events others have experienced. To the contrary, I empathize totally, but here is another take on it that has shaped the entrepreneur I have become today and provided a foundation for success going forward.

I wanted to give you some value in this short chapter—points of reference if you will—that have shaped who I have become since those awkward days as a high school drop-out and teenage mum.

Recently, a mentor shared a quote that has been responsible for the most recent pivot in my entrepreneur journey.

"Maybe the journey isn't so much about becoming anything. Maybe it's about un-becoming everything that isn't really you, so you can be who you were meant to be in the first place."

To most of us who would be reading this book, the "un-becoming" speaks of our true identity. If you've ever asked yourself the question, *Who am I?* then you'll appreciate what I share here.

Our life experiences, good and bad, shape who we become over time, layer upon layer of what we tell ourselves, both consciously and unconsciously and how the 'unbecoming' can serve you as well.

You've likely already "arrived" as an entrepreneur. At the very least, you're on your way. You have the entrepreneur DNA. The next phase of this journey is about letting go of all the things that keep us small—that keep us safe and the same. What we tell ourselves has the potential to limit us and also has the power to make us stronger, more resilient, and more successful. It's a conscious choice.

Now, back to where this all began—the wild skydiving adventure. It wasn't a case of thrill-seeking (okay, maybe just a little). I was looking for adventure, and the opportunity came up when a group of guys from the surf club wanted to go skydiving. It was on my bucket list, so I paid up my money and secured my spot.

We spent the day training. We learned how to roll when we landed and how to field pack our chutes afterward. There were thirteen jumpers, and I was the only girl. I wanted to be the first that jumped that day, but the instructor said no. I was to go last—number thirteen. I'm not sure if this is significant enough to mention, but I will for fun. All the helmets had names on them. As if the number thirteen wasn't a clear enough message, mine was labeled Goose. If you've seen the movie *Top Gun*, then you know it was a message that I clearly ignored.

I was so pumped for the jump. We crawled to the back of the plane and sat there until we were told to move toward the open door, one at a time. With hearts racing, we kept our eyes glued on the instructor who would give the thumbs-up. I crawled out onto the wing strut of the plane and looked to the instructor for the thumbs-up to let go. I remember thinking I really wanted to go to the toilet just then, but I instantly dismissed the thought. Yep, I was going to make that jump. There was a brief moment when I thought, *This is nuts, why am I doing this?* But it was a fleeting thought. I got the signal from the instructor, and I let go. "One thousand, two thousand, three thousand, four thousand, five thousand, Geronimo!" I heard myself scream as the chute opened.

We jumped under round army chutes, and at that time, there was no wind. It's what they call a "still wind landing." I crashed to the ground rather dramatically with no wind in my chute to enable me to take the roll. The impact spiral fractured the tibia and fibula bones in my right leg and dislocated the ankle. After three months of non-weight-bearing healing and a total of three surgeries over the years came the good news—I could walk. Every day, I plant my feet firmly on the ground when I get out of bed and look to my feet, grateful that I have them.

When I need to make a decision to take the next leap, I relive that day in the plane. I gather the same courage and take that leap. I step out knowing full well that I may fail, but I also know how to pick myself up, dust off, and do it again the next day, regardless of the outcome.

"The willingness to show up changes us; it makes us a little braver each time."

—Brene Brown

I didn't know it at the time, but this life lesson, learned early in my career, would serve me well down the track as I learned to apply my craft as an entrepreneur in the online world.

I set about on what seemed an impossible journey at the time. I gained entry into teachers college as a mature student at twenty-two. Childcare was not a thing back then, so my daughter, Sandy, at the ripe age of two, became the youngest trainee teacher. She sat alongside me for three years with her colored pencils and paper in more psych lectures than most registered students. It was a question of time-tabling, contact time at college, study, and juggling life as a single mum. I learned that the only way I was going to graduate was to show up at lectures, contribute, and get noticed by my tutors. That wasn't hard with the cutest toddler on campus in tow—in fact, she was the only toddler on campus. I took on the role of student councilor and editor of the college magazine. It gave me status, authority, and contributed to the student body. I knew intuitively that would be important.

Leadership as an entrepreneur is a given. If you don't think you're a leader, then think again. I had more support through those years from tutors and other students than I have ever experienced since that time.

To this day, I show up to everything possible and soak up the lessons. It doesn't matter if it's a family event, another Zoom call with my tribe, or an industry event. I never falter. I am always there—the most reliable student in the room. The difference is that now I have developed a filter to take in only what matters in the moment, what I need *now* to finish what I am working on.

At college, I took endless pages of notes so I could study at home. There was no computer, so everything was handwritten. At night, after the kids were tucked in, I would study the notes I'd taken into the wee hours. I maintain this same practice today. I was driven to succeed even though I had no idea what that might look like. I had 100% attendance throughout those years. At the time, I didn't know the value of handwritten notes and the connection to the brain. Today I still handwrite my notes; I have endless notebooks of priceless content. I never show up without a pad and pen. It's how I learn, how I lock away those gold nuggets to regurgitate when I'm coaching or teaching. How do you learn? What system have you adopted that works for you?

"If you believe you can or believe you can't, you're right."
—Henry Ford

For the longest time, I have been challenged with Imposter Syndrome and feelings of not being enough. From a very young age, I have felt that whatever I do will never be enough. Being constantly told what I could *not* do has just made me more focused on what I can achieve. "You're a mother. You can't do that. Who will look after the kids?" Never mind, I'll take them with me. My daughter sat in the coach's speed dinghy at 4:00 a.m., rugged up while I occupied my place in the rowing crew. There was nothing traditional about how I raised my kids, that's for sure.

It's a daily work in progress to think above the line—to stay accountable, take ownership, and be responsible for everything I do and say. One of the first success principles of coaching that I learned was cause and effect. I remember how significant that was to me at the time.

*"Are you the type of person who is the cause of things that happen in your life, or are you at the effect of things that happen to you? Which is more empowering? To be **at** cause or to be **at** effect?"*

One of my personal affirmations reads, "I am at cause for everything I say and do." In overcoming some of the challenges in my life, this has been a fundamental principle. To be an effective coach, I live my message daily.

"We are the average of the five people we spend the most time with."

—Jim Rohn

One of the most valuable aspects of entrepreneurialism is the power of the tribe. It's been a lifesaver to me on this journey of self-discovery. I choose my tribe carefully, knowing the power of this quote. Over the years, I have drifted away from some of the acquaintances who have influenced my life, and in the past, even family members.

Three years ago, I made a serious commitment to research how to take my coaching business online. I was making six figures comfortably, but I had grown disillusioned by the one-to-one coaching model. It was the dirty little secret of the coaching industry that there was no way to scale beyond six figures when you were trading time for money. Digital space scaling *one to many* seemed like it was the right answer, but I had no idea where to start or who to follow. So, I prepared for yet another leap from a perfectly good airplane and jumped right out. I could have never prepared for what I would find in this dimension. Every day was a new rabbit hole to dive into. First stop was Russell Brunson and Click Funnels, where I would follow a bright young millennial, Steve Larsen, into the funnel abyss.

Today, I have launched my new online coaching platform, Strategic Pearls Coaching. Life is good once again. I'm stronger and more ready for the next chapter of trials, life events, challenges, and fun times. Bring on adversity, for then I know I am alive.

The real adversity to overcome is to conquer what holds you back—the fears, limiting beliefs, and all the "stuff" we collect along the way. This is true for me and has been more challenging to overcome than any specific life event. Imposter Syndrome and the feeling of not being enough can be paralyzing.

I don't mind sharing that, until recently, I have thought of myself as more the marathon runner or long-distance gal that never gives up. However, there is a new breed on the horizon, and they take no prisoners. If you wait until it's perfect, they'll run over the top of you. Take massive action daily. "Done" is the new perfect. Fail hard and fail fast, get up, dust off, and go again. Get your mindset on the positive loop, become above-the-line accountable, take ownership, and be responsible for everything that happens in your life.

See your future now.

ABOUT TONI BARNETT

Toni is a certified life and business coach. She lives and works between Perth, Western Australia, and Bali, Indonesia. A solopreneur since her early twenties, Toni founded Corporate Focus, her first entrepreneurial endeavor, a sports marketing and event management business that partnered not-for-profit sports organizations with corporate sponsors.

As a teenage mum at seventeen, Toni raised her kids as a single parent. Today, she is an enthusiastic nanna to an extended, blended tribe. She is passionate about education and personal growth for youth and is an active advocate for change in our education system to better prepare our little ones for what lies ahead.

For over two decades, Toni has partnered with her husband Neil as a hotel broker in his real estate and business agency, specializing in hospitality sales, marketing, and management.

Today, Toni is living her passion. She empowers working mums who are juggling life, kids, and relationships, challenging them to step out and craft an abundant lifestyle that better meets their needs and gives them freedom to choose. She also coaches executive women in leadership inside her Pearls of Change Challenge program.

"All good things start with family."

www.StrategicPearlsCoaching.com
info@StrategicPearls.com

KEEP YOUR MIND ON THE GROOVE

by Bradley Rapier

I had just hung up the phone after a conversation with an executive from MTV. Sitting there in silence, I questioned my decision. This wasn't the first time.

It was the fall of 2008, and for the third season in a row, I had turned down prominent national television opportunities from two major networks. On paper, they were solid matches for our collective crew, but I continued to hold out for something else that I held in my heart and could see in my mind.

As *The Groovaloos*, we already had a number of significant achievements under our belt: *American Street Dance Champions*, first dance company chosen as special guests on *So You Think You Can Dance*, multiple featured appearances on *The Wayne Brady Show*, and breaking box office records with the premiere of our autobiographical stage show, *GROOVALOO*. However, substantial success came to those that took the new opportunities I had passed up. While I held out for some elusive vision, doubts in my leadership and decision-making abilities grew, even within my own mind. To compound matters, *The Groovaloos* and the other groups that had taken those opportunities now had a number of common members in their ranks with conflicting commitments. The challenge became twofold; how to continue to believe and hold on to a vision amidst growing confusion while still keeping individual members connected to that vision as other enticing opportunities began coming their way. I had to keep my mind on the groove, regardless of how my moves continued to be in question.

146

It was just a decade earlier that my wife and I started the informal get-togethers on the rooftop of our Hollywood apartment. The gatherings stemmed from a desire for community and centered around music, food, and a lot of dance, particularly hip hop and freestyle. These *Groove Nites'* became a weekly happening after moving them to a dance studio in the Valley. As bonds grew, they attracted a mix of some of the best talent from Los Angeles with legends of street dance culture.

Groove Nite was strengthened by the fact that at that time there was very little access available to this type of setting outside of a night club. Dancers traveled from all over to train and be a part of what was taking place. It was from this backdrop of relationships that *The Groovaloos* were formed and became a prominent fixture in L.A., loudly introducing ourselves with an explosive finalé performance at *National Dance Day* in 1999. Our infectious celebration of freestyle dance, combined with our unique approach to bringing all street styles together, had a rippling effect on the culture. The crew grew and exploded on the hip hop dance scene. *Groove Nite* and *The Groovaloos* became a launching pad for untold numbers of prominent dancers and choreographers.

Personally, it was a surreal time for me. In my native country of Canada, the dance had a magical quality to it as we created larger than life characters out of the legends we heard about. As a bright-eyed young man, I had been swept up into the incredible power and freedom behind the art form that I was helping to pioneer. The result was a drastic change in the direction of my life. It led me down to the United States, where I was then surrounded by street dance culture at the highest level. It affected me and my love of story so deeply, I believed the dance could reach the world in a new way.

My desire was to give others a glimpse of the greatness I was experiencing, beyond videos and street performances and into the heart of the culture upon stages it had not reached before. But a big hurdle existed within the art form itself. So much of the beauty of hip hop lives in its freestyle component. The ability to connect to the groove and authentically release inspired creative movement in the moment is something not designed for duplication. In an industry that regularly demands perfect replication of specific moves at specific times, the idea of presenting exhilarating but unpredictable outcomes of real freestyle was a road less traveled. It would require a fresh template and some marketplace innovation. I was all in.

I began pitching dance competition shows to networks in the pre-*So You Think You Can Dance* days, with *The Groovaloos* providing a soulful backdrop as individual freestyle dance challenges were combined with group competitions. I wrote a musical with fictional characters that would allow freestyle qualities to shine within a magical "small-town boy takes on the big city" story. We had producers attached and a fantastic combination of talented artists and dancers to help present our industry showcases. The projects were gaining momentum when something happened out of left field that turned things upside down.

The *Groovaloos* were in the middle of taping a series of "how to hip hop" instructional videos. The producer informed me that we had an extra thirty minutes to fill. I decided to interview the members on why they came to L.A. and what drew them to the company. I was expecting answers to focus on the joy of dance and going for the Hollywood dream, but that was not what I got. The actual responses carried much more weight: "I would not exist without this dance... I would be in jail... this is how I survived the abuse of my father." The answers took my breath away.

Deeply impacted, I took the voiceovers from the interviews into the editing room and matched them with b-roll of each specific dancer. The result was powerful. I immediately invited a few members of *The Groovaloos* and my talented director friend, Danny Cistone, over to my place. The response was unanimous, "We have a real show." Danny and I went to work assembling interviews into a narrative. We collaborated with *The Groovaloos* as we developed story content and worked with member Charlie "Vzion8" Schmidt to bring key aspects of freestyle culture to life through his dynamic, spoken-word poetry. The question then became where to present this concept.

The Groovaloos had gained favor at the main industry dance event in Hollywood called *The Choreographers Carnival*, a monthly showcase of top choreographers and dancers. At the time, *Carnival* had no rival, and we had become a staple performing group of the production. I approached *Carnival* producer Carey Ysais about *The Groovaloos* taking over a night. We were friends, but I believe his exact words were, "You›re crazy, bro!" You see, on any given month the *Carnival* has about two hundred dancers and twenty choreographers presenting twenty or more individual choreographed numbers. We were one group, and I was asking for the entire evening. It took some serious selling, but Carey finally gave in to my passionate pleas. He offered us one hour of stage time. We made that hour count.

The venue was packed as *An Evening with the Groovaloos* made its debut on the Sunset Strip in 2003. The dance community flooded the first floor as agents, celebrities, and recording artists crowded around tables up on the balcony. The result was overwhelming. Dancers were left in tears, sharing how the show reminded them why they came to L.A. and why they dance. Celebrities and fellow choreographers showered us with praise. But it was my agent, Julie McDonald, who summarized it best. She spoke firmly into my ear as the DJ blared music in the background, "Bradley! Stop everything you are doing and do this!" I knew she was right. There was promise in the other projects being developed, but this show had massive potential to share profound elements behind freestyle culture, all wrapped within the framework of unique, authentic stories. The larger story blended the spirit of family and the pursuit of meaning and identity we all face in life. It carried so much of the vision I was believing for, but in the land of film and TV, what did it actually mean to develop a theater show of this type? There was no playbook. In a culture not aligned with freestyle patterns, this would require me to keep my mind on that groove.

Along the unique process of developing *GROOVALOO*, there were many wild moments, opportunities, and struggles. We navigated through movie meetings, TV series discussions, and multiple Broadway proposals and workshops. There was tremendous creative excitement but also a significant amount of external pressure to change the show. Working to keep the larger vision in sight, I was often placed in the middle, trying to find common ground between outside producers and *The Groovaloos*. At times these internal strains came dangerously close to causing irreparable relational damage within our company. On top of this challenge, short-term goals were quickly becoming increasingly handicapped by a scheduling nightmare. Demand for individual members outside of our crew activity grew as *Groovaloos* became stand-outs in national commercial campaigns, A-list music tours, and dance films. But the toughest challenge actually happened early on in the process. Between our debut on Sunset Strip and presenting our first set of theater presentations, one of our founding members, who played a lead role in our stage play, was critically injured.

Steven "Boogieman" Stanton was celebrating at a night club with his students after teaching dance workshops when two rival gangs entered and engaged in a deadly shoot out. Thankfully, Steven survived, but bullets penetrated his lower spine. He was the most severely injured of those who lived. As I hopped on a plane to see him, I remember thinking, what does keeping my mind on the groove have to do with any of this right now? One of my best friends has suffered a serious tragedy, and I've been focused on a stage show.

Prior to entering his hospital room, I was informed that with his injury, it was very unlikely Steven would ever walk again, let alone dance. The gravity of the situation, along with all that had been happening, took my emotions to the edge. However, as I stood beside Steven's bed and hinted that I was considering letting go of the show, without a pause, he set me straight. "No! What you are building is bigger than me—and I'll kick your butt if you do." He then gave me that sarcastic smile of his, and I had

150

to laugh. Amazingly enough, it was Steven who would be able to keep his mind locked clearly on the groove, even when faced with the most challenging obstacles of all.

Miraculously, it was Steven's story that would be the crucial element to bring the production together. Contrary to the doctor's predictions, Steven never agreed with the diagnosis. His faith and personal outlook only saw himself recovering. As we workshopped ideas to complete the story, it became clear that the concept of not being able to do what you believe you were designed to do was a pivotal question of *GROOVALOO*. Who are you if you are not able to pursue what you've come to believe is your destiny? This became the climax of the show, bringing Steven back to the stage in an unforgettably impactful return.

Within my coaching on the *Groove Mindset*, I have a saying, "*It's not the move; it's the groove.*" Open your eyes to what speaks to your core, guides you to where you are headed, and reinforces all that you stand for. Challenges and opportunities along the way are part of the process, but they should not become the focus. They are moves. Moves that either prepare you or propel you toward what lies ahead in your journey as you connect to the larger groove.

One of the key lines in *GROOVALOO* spoken by Steven reflects that specific thought, "*Life isn't always choreographed. Sometimes you have to freestyle.*" This encapsulates the heart of freestyle in dance and in life. You will always run out of moves, but the groove is endless.

And that brings us full circle to the phone conversation with the executive in 2008. Up to that time, we had been building the crew and presenting *GROOVALOO* in Los Angeles as our flagship production. We had a solid presence in the community with previous national television exposure, and our stage show had been booked into the prestigious Orange County Performing Arts Center.

A new TV show had been launched titled *America's Best Dance Crew*. The phone call was the third time they had asked me to present a faction of *The Groovaloos* for the show. The production generated a great deal of excitement, but it was the format that I couldn't get past. Routines were sixty seconds in length with six performers. We had a large group with multiple styles, and with our particular approach to dance culture, in sixty seconds, we would just be getting into a groove. I didn't see a match for what I was envisioning.

In the first season, after I turned down the request, two members of *The Groovaloos* let me know they were going to audition for the show with other dancers. That other group was *The JabbaWockeez*. This repeated two more seasons with *SuperCr3w* and *The Beatfreaks*, where between them there were seven members from *The Groovaloos*.

Within this time, I also received a call from *America's Got Talent*. Again, sixty second routines where we might be challenged by someone who balances bowling balls on their nose. I just couldn't see the groove in that. But the success these shows were bringing to the contestants was undeniable. Our stage show was stalling; we seemed to be in a circular pattern of meetings that were not moving the needle. To add to all this, my agent called with one more TV show proposal.

The show was being produced by Nigel Lythgoe and Simon Fuller and called *Superstars of Dance*. The premise was promising. The series would be an Olympic-scale international competition with eight countries vying for the world title. *The Groovaloos* had been chosen to represent the United States, which positioned us as champions on the national level. The show format would allow us to have up to ten members, include story and spoken-word poetry, and best of all, dance routines would be three to four minutes in length! For reality television, that was unheard of. A decisive "*Yes, we accept!*" came out of my lips fairly quickly this time around.

The 2009 premiere of *Superstars of Dance* was one of the highest-rated NBC shows outside of a sporting event and was described as one the greatest spectacles of dance performance ever seen on television. The process was grueling, but it was a truly amazing experience. We consistently won over judges and viewers alike with our theatrical take on hip hop dance culture. *The Groovaloos* and team USA brought the championship trophy home in front of millions. It was an emotional time and a great honor for us. For me, the moment was wonderfully overwhelming. We were able to present a solid reflection of our groove.

Just as we rode the groove to this great height, more unbelievable news came. A New York producer was making plans to take *GROOVALOO* to the Big Apple. *The Groovaloos* went on to play *Off-Broadway* and tour nationally. It was incredibly gratifying to provide an atmosphere that allowed the performers to fully express themselves within the freestyle culture at the highest level. We had overcome the battle to fit into the established model. This cemented a legacy and a movement for all *The Groovaloos,* set in motion by our shared groove all those years ago.

There have been many adventures since then and plenty of times on my groove journey where I made mountains out of moves. Thankfully, I had a wife in my corner and a full inner circle of crew members that freestyled with me into the unknown. The longer the journey and the deeper the trust of the groove, the more breathtaking and unexpected support I have found from others along the way. On this road of entrepreneurship, you have got to see the larger vision as you deal with pressure and your own self-doubts. Now, I see nothing but new ventures. Ventures to be reached and explored with others, as we keep our minds on the groove.

ABOUT BRADLEY RAPIER

Twenty years ago, Bradley pioneered a movement in Los Angeles that ignited the community and positively impacted the landscape for hip hop and freestyle dance in culture and media. Now, using his dynamic life experiences and powerful analogies from the art form, Bradley guides audiences into the circle of *Groove Theory* to break people free from self-doubt, anxiety, fear, and disconnectedness. Through discovery and activation sessions, he opens eyes and minds while taking individuals and teams down new pathways to a *Groove Mindset*. This *Groove Mindset* speaks to all areas of life and reveals higher levels of creativity, authenticity, and freedom. Bradley and his wife live in Los Angeles and have three beautiful children. Credits include; *La La Land, Dancing With The Stars, So You Think You Can Dance, Ellen, World of Dance, Superstars of Dance,* and *Jesus Christ Superstar.* Awards include *Ovation, World Dance,* and *NAACP.* He is the founder of *The Groovaloos.*

http://bradleyrapier.com
@bradleyrapier
@groovemindset
@groovaloos

MY JOURNEY FROM NOTHING TO $100,000 IN DEBT TO A SIX-FIGURE INCOME

by Joanna Mak

Adversity will be your constant or occasional companion throughout your life. You cannot avoid it. The only question is how you will act or react to it. Will your adversities be stumbling blocks or stepping stones? The gift of moral agency empowers you to choose how you will act when you suffer adversity.

Here was my journey in understanding adversity and the lesson I learned. Growing up, there were not many things I considered adversities. Not until 1992 when my husband and I both graduated from college and had our first child. His first month's salary was $1,500. After taxes, rent, health insurance, and tithing, there was no money left for diapers or other basic necessities.

We prayed hard and then saw the opportunity of running our produce business. A lot of people came to buy the off-grade bananas from the produce company he worked for. Instead of paying $20 for 50 pounds of A-grade bananas, they bought the $5 off-grade bananas. Without any money, we started our produce business by borrowing $500 from a church member as the down payment for our truck, and my husband borrowed the balance from his brothers and sisters.

Selling produce was quite an experience. Every Friday morning, my husband bought the produce and parked his truck before he went to work. I carried around 35 to 50 boxes of 50-pound crates of produce and walked up to our second-story apartment.

I weighted them, bagged them, and packed them back into the same box. My son was around six months old, and he would grab a potato or anything to bite on while I was busy packing. How painful and guilty I felt toward my baby! Instead of holding him, playing, or reading to him, I was busy holding a whole bunch of produce just to survive.

After a day of hard labor and feeling totally exhausted, I carried boxes of produce, walked down another two stories, and put them back into the truck. I felt pity for myself for a while, but I reminded myself that it was all right to be broke temporarily, and I had to do whatever it took to get myself out of this situation. Adversities are temporary, too. What is permanent is what we become from the way we react to them.

On Saturday morning, we would drive one hour to our college town and sold produce to the whole community. In the beginning, I feared and cared about what other people would think about me. The image of me, a college graduate selling produce like the ladies in the market or in China Town horrified me. I had to throw away my pride, my ego, my image, and my self-esteem to stand there selling produce. Later, I became very good at it, and I realized I was serving people. I overcame my mental block, and I was grateful for having a lot of happy customers. It was quite a scene to see a whole bunch of my customers actually lining up, waiting for, and welcoming me every Saturday. They thanked me because they didn't have to spend the whole Saturday morning to drive to town to buy produce. I offered fresher, cheaper varieties of produce for them. My business saved them time and money. They loved me for that. Years later, my clients still remember me as the produce lady.

It was a very profitable business for me at that time. I prided myself for earning more money than my husband by only working one-and-a-half days a week. Honestly, I really appreciated my husband. Without his help and support, I couldn't have started my produce business.

Starting with nothing and unable to support ourselves to starting my first business, this experience always gives me the confidence and the belief that I can always figure things out. Opportunities are everywhere; you just have to pay attention and look for opportunities. I overcame my first financial adversity and got the blessing of starting my entrepreneur journey. I also become physically, mentally, and spiritually strong.

Things were going well for a while, but then I faced my second adversity. I was forced to separate from my husband, leave Hawaii, and abandon my business. The reason I was not allowed to work in the United States and eventually had to go back to Hong Kong was that I was out of status for a couple of months when I was pregnant. The security guard at the immigration department didn't understand my situation and refused to let me in to file my change-of-status paperwork. I ended up separating from my husband for a couple of years.

I was not able to live on my own, so I lived with my parents in Hong Kong. Feeling lonely, depending on others, and not knowing about our future, all because of the ignorance of that security guard. During those years, my son didn't have the chance to see his father, and my husband couldn't watch his son growing up. The security guard's words and actions imposed such a significant negative impact on our family. Did I blame the security guard for my years of separating from my husband and the hardship that I had raising my son alone? I didn't.

In life, sometimes your tribulations and afflictions are caused by choices of your own, such as making the wrong decision, going to the wrong places, or hanging out with the wrong people. They may be the results of the poor choices of the people around you or even strangers. In my case, it was the security guard. The last one was a natural disaster.

However, no matter what happens, you have the absolute agency to choose how to handle adversities. You can remain positive and find a solution to fix the problem, or you can choose to be negative and blame others or circumstances for your suffering. Even though you have the freedom to choose your actions, you can't choose the consequences of your action. I remind myself to look for the good out of any adversity. Complaining and murmuring don't help with anything. It turned out to be a blessing that I could stay with my parents for couples of years because my son developed a relationship with my parents. Later on, I returned to Hawaii and reunited with my husband. My second son was born in 1996.

In 1997, when Hong Kong was returning back to China, my husband and I made the decision to move back to Hong Kong. After two months, he went back to Hawaii to help his previous company move, not knowing that his boss just filed for bankruptcy. After discussing it with me, he made the choice to hire the whole operation team, pick up the business, and start his own company while I was in Hong Kong helping my brother with his business with a two-year commitment.

Those two years went by fast. In 1999, I returned to Hawaii, and I was shocked to find that the company was $100,000 in debt in payroll taxes and other credit card charges. I quickly realized that there were too many employees, and the sales manager was not performing. All the income went to the employees, and there was nothing left for us, and we were in the red for months.

My husband was very nice to his employees. He would rather suffer himself than not pay his employees. He was charging his own credit card and paying an extremely high interest rate to pay the employees. He even wanted to give the sales manager a second chance to perform and gave him a quota. Instead of performing, he ended up stealing and erasing our client database, opening his own company, and taking our clients and competing against us. He actually opened his company behind our back doing the same business we did and used our secretary doing promotion for his company way before we fired him. After he got fired, he spread bad rumors about us. The saddest thing was that sometimes we met him at events, and he totally ignored us and treated us as if we didn't exist. I should have felt being betrayed and taken advantage of by someone whom we trusted. It was really unbelievable, but I felt sorry for him. I asked myself, *Why should I let* him *decide how I'm going to act and feel?* I chose to forgive, forget, and move on with my life.

I learned a great lesson from this incident. I didn't allow those negative feelings, hatred, or victim mentality to poison my mind and my soul. I couldn't afford to let the negativity build up and drown me, turning me into a person whom I didn't want to become. I chose to let go of the bad feeling towards the sales manager, and direct and channel my energy to work on my business. I had total control over how to handle the challenge. Over and over, we are hurt deeply by people whom we love or trust either intentionally or unintentionally. Do I have to lose faith on people? I have to remind myself over and over that people are imperfect; they make mistakes just like me. I don't let people, circumstances, misfortune, or any other so-called reason stop me from becoming my best self.

Adversity is like a furnace of fire to refine you and make you be your best self. I also always remember the tender mercy of my Heavenly Father who loves and forgives my weaknesses and mistakes. He expects me to love and forgive others as He does. What a joyful feeling if you can put down the burden of hatred and even love those who hurt and even persecute you!

When we are faced with the toughest times, those are the moments we are tested with based on what kind of choices we make. Our choices reveal our character and define who we are. We are commanded to be like Jesus Christ and to love one another. Whenever I face adversity or difficulties, I will always look to my Savior who is my strength and my role model. He taught me how to be courageous and keep my standard no matter what happens or how hard it gets. My affliction is so small compared with what he went through. No one in this earth would ever experience the intensity of pain, anguish, loneliness, and suffering as he went through. Our suffering is only for a small moment, even though it feels like an eternity for most people. Always look to Him, and He will give you strength and comfort and help you overcome all adversities.

After the drama, I need to restructure my company. There was no way for our company to survive. I made the hardest business decision to let go of all of our seven employees in phases. Once again, I had to do the one thing that I absolutely hated the most: borrowing money from my brothers and sisters. At the same time, I took on the job of my seven employees. Only I and my husband were left to run the company.

In one year, I paid off all debt, turned the company around, and started earning a six-figure income year after year. But it was not done without a price. I worked extremely hard, and I didn't get to go home until 10:00 or 11:00 p.m. for many years. My husband would take the kids home and cook dinner for them while I would stay behind to work until I was super tired. It started all over the next day. I didn't have a life at all. Most of the time, we couldn't attend our children's activities at school, and we hardly had time for vacations or any family events. Somehow, I realized I didn't own a business—my business owned me. I had created a never-ending job for myself. It paid well in the beginning, but I was only trading my time for money. We did not have the time freedom and financial freedom that we wanted, which was defeating the purpose of why we got into running the business in the first place.

Looking back, if I knew the marketing skills, strategies, and tactics that I do right now; I could easily have turned the company around, not by lowering my expenses by letting my employees go, but by generating a constant flow of customers and increasing revenue. I didn't have to do everything myself. I could be the true CEO of my company, making important decision working *on* my business and not *in* my business. Happily, I now own my business, and never let my business own me.

All the experiences I cumulated as an accountant, a business owner, a realtor, and a digital marketer helped me understand the challenges that most businesses go through. My adversity journey ignites my entrepreneurial spirit and propels me to find solutions to my problems. From all my adversities, I feel for the people who have the same or similar challenges as me. They are trading their health, time, relationships, and even their dreams for money. I felt their frustrations, pain, and helplessness. I found that my greatest joy is sharing what I know and lessening the pain of others as much as I can. The courageous faith and action of someone who excels in handling adversity can be a great blessing to others who are strengthened by the example. I was inspired by many, and I wish to inspire many.

In conclusion, don't dwell on the adversity and ask why it happened to you. Things do not happen *to* you; they happen *for* you. Look for the good that comes out of your adversity and give thanks. Count your blessings every day and have a heart full of gratitude. Choose to be happy. There are many people who had situations worse than yours. Never lose hope, never give up. Look up, reach out, and create your own destiny. Enjoy and live your life to its fullest and give back in return. The world will be a better place because you overcome adversities and show the world what is possible.

ABOUT JOANNA MAK

Joanna Mak is the founder and CEO of Digital Clouds Marketing Solutions. She takes a forensic approach to analyzing, designing, and automating her client's marketing campaigns to increase profits, visibility, and time freedom. She is passionate about empowering business owners to be a true CEO, enjoying both financial and time freedom. Her mission of giving highly personalized advice focused on building wealth by increasing profits, keeping more profits, and ultimately multiplying profits through digital marketing, asset protection, tax strategies, real estate investing, and accessing her wealth network.

Her diverse experience in accounting, running her convention rental business, and being a realtor and real estate investor helps her take a comprehensive and strategic approach to build a long-term and profitable business. As an integrated marketer, she innovates and discovers new ways and technologies to leverage the tools to create profitable products and programs that deepened and solidify customer relationships to build brands and awareness.

Born and raised in Hong Kong, she attended BYU-Hawaii. She loves playing badminton, table tennis, and karaoke. She loves singing, traveling, reading, and building businesses and people at the same time.

digitalcloudsmarketingsolutions.com

AT ALL COSTS—DO NOT QUIT!

by Aaron Janda

"When obstacles arise, you change your direction to reach your goal;
you do not change your decision to get there."

—Zig Ziglar

A strange sense of calm came over me one July evening as I laid down on our bed. I laid there for a while, trying to calculate, figure out, and question the decisions made over the last six months leading up to that point. I looked at other people's choices, decisions, actions, and reactions, as well as my own. Although I had a level of peace and calm, I did have the overwhelming temptation to ask, *Why me?*

Statistically, by the age of thirty-nine, everyone will have at least one polarizing life event that has the potential to either make or break them. I had four of them back-to-back in a very short period of time, and it nearly derailed me and my business career. I had a business partner steal upwards of $250,000 in royalties. Six months after those payments ceased, I lost a family member to cancer.

When I arrived home from that trip, I found that my wife had left me. She was also threatening to sue me for a business I had just spent the previous six months building. It was a relationship that ultimately ended in divorce. A few short months after the separation, I had two lawsuits filed against me for bad debts based on other people's decisions and actions. The silver lining in all of it is—I have a story to tell! It's a story that may help someone else who is up against what may seem to be impossible circumstances. In my two upcoming books, *Your Story Matters* and *Don't Quit,* I will be sharing more about how to overcome those types of situations. You'll also hear from some other individuals who've been through even more extreme life events.

As we look at *Overcoming Adversity in Entrepreneurship* through the lenses of different individuals throughout this book, one theme rings true throughout: anyone embarking on the journey of a lifetime in entrepreneurship must have several things—grit, tenacity, perseverance, and definitely, a *don't quit* attitude, no matter what the cost. I want to look at what entrepreneurship is in a general sense and what you may encounter along the way.

When I think of entrepreneurship, I think of individuals who don't settle for the status quo. I think of individuals who don't want to settle for society's expectations or opinions of what their life should look like.

I have always been very independent. Thinking back to my childhood, I always managed to find odd jobs to make money. First, I traded and sold baseball cards. At the age of fifteen, I got my first official job at McDonald's. I then saved up enough money to buy my first car at sixteen. I didn't wait for any handouts or for anyone to give me anything.

I went on to work at my next job for several years, ultimately leaving with not much to show for it. I then transitioned to another job for four-and-a-half years, leaving that job only to transition to yet another job for four *more* years. I'm sure the upward progress looked pretty good on a resumé, but I wasn't any closer to my personal life goals.

I had an epiphany. I realized that I'd spent half of my life working the "nine-to-five" without getting any closer to achieving my life goals. I worked day-in and day-out just to pay bills and make other people wealthy, while I had very little to show for it. Then something happened.

After working half of my life for other people, I had the opportunity to start my own business in Seattle, WA. At the age of 30—what some would consider a late start—I launched my first business remodeling kitchen cabinets. I incorporated the business, signed up for a 10' x 10' booth at the Seattle Home Show, and was off to the races. I was able to build the business into a six-figure income in my first year.

On the one hand, I had felt extremely blessed where I was at, but on the other hand, I felt like I had been duped—duped by a system that was not advantageous enough to create the life most people would want for themselves.

I realized very quickly that if I was going to create the life I wanted, it was going to happen because I made the decision to create value for others. I knew that if I could create enough value for enough people, the income would follow. Zig Ziglar said, "*You will get what you want in life, if you help enough people get what they want.*"

It wouldn't be forthright to not tell you that creating the life you want for you and your family will not come without its fair share of obstacles. Most people view entrepreneurship as a life filled with private travel, countless days on the beach, endless margaritas, and an American Express Black Card to pay for it all. While it can include some of those things, it definitely does not start there.

The truth of the matter is, most entrepreneurs' journeys include experiences that would make the average person shudder. I have two good friends who've both had multiple millions stolen from them by rogue business partners. Both individuals had to start completely over after losing everything. One person I know was indicted for fraud but was never charged because his partners were found guilty of stealing money from the business. Another entrepreneur friend of mine was sued by a large computer company (who will remain nameless) for close to forty million dollars. Could you even imagine being in that position? Fortunately, he was able to defend himself and ended up winning, but it would have been impossible without his tenacity and unrelenting attitude to not give up at any cost.

Money is a very funny thing, indeed. We need money to live, and it does make the world go 'round, but money in and of itself is neutral. Money is neither good nor bad. Conversely, how we obtain it can be either good or bad. Statistically, 90% of crimes committed in the U.S. are money motivated.

Money is great at revealing a person's character. If you're a jerk now with very little money, you'll just become a bigger jerk if you obtain a large sum of it. If you're a sincere, genuine, caring, and giving person now, then when you come into larger sums of money, it will magnify those qualities, and it will be obvious to those around you.

Unfortunately, in the world of entrepreneurship, I'm finding that business partners going rogue is not an uncommon occurrence. They'll steal large sums of money or abandon ship, leaving you holding your hands in the air with a mountain of debt and knocking on bankruptcy's door. Entrepreneurship can be the most rewarding adventure, but it's definitely not for the faint of heart. If you're an entrepreneur or desire to be one, you most likely have an overwhelming sense of purpose. You're probably someone who wants to make a difference in the world that is much bigger than yourself, and for that I commend you. If you go for it, and most definitely *Do Not Quit,* I believe you can, and you will. If that's your motive, then regardless of the challenges and obstacles you may face, it will most definitely be worth it!

ABOUT AARON JANDA

Aaron Janda is a two-time Amazon bestselling author, inspirational speaker, and serial entrepreneur. Aaron authored his first book *My $100 Dollar Project*, a book that challenges readers to take $100 and multiply it to $1,000 and beyond. Aaron co-authored his second book, *Influence and Income Online*, which became an Amazon #1 bestseller in five categories.

Aaron has launched multiple six-figure businesses. He had lost everything and had to rebuild his life and business for a third time. He will be sharing more of his story in his two upcoming books, *Your Story Matters* and *Don't Quit*. Aaron is passionate about helping others and sharing his story in hopes that it can help someone who is facing what may seem to be impossible circumstances. If you would like to book Aaron to speak at your school or event, contact him for more info at the email below.

Aaron is also the founder of Legacy Publishing Co., a publishing company whose three core values are to:

1. Maximize the platform for entrepreneurs, influencers, and anyone else who wants to leave a lasting impact on the world.
2. Fund projects to help those who are not able to help themselves.
3. Create generational wealth to leave a lasting legacy for generations to come. If you have a story to tell, Aaron would love to give you a free book consultation!

If you would like any more information about how Aaron can add value to your business or organization, contact him directly at
info@aaronjanda.com
aaronjanda.com
legacypublishingco.com

THE DAY I BOUGHT A BUSINESS AND LOST EVERYTHING

by Susan Jones

F inally, I was eye to eye with this man again.

I was angry. So angry that I was shaking. Angry with him. Angry with our lawyers. Angry with the whole situation.

I wanted him to know a few things.

How much money we had lost—almost everything we had built through years of hard work. I wanted him to know that we had had to sell our property portfolio to pay back the debts he had caused us to incur, that his "employee" had taken us to the small claims tribunal, that we had had to disconnect our phone because of all the calls from people who were upset with *him*.

I wanted him to know that I was angry that he lied to us and forged Rob's signature. That he had caused six months of unbearable stress while we fought him through the courts. That this had been the hardest thing we had ever had to cope with.

How I wished I could tell him what I really thought.

But I didn't get to say any of this.

He sat there, brazen as brass, not sorry a bit, while I fumed. The lawyers were doing their thing, and there was no place for me to tell him anything.

But I can tell you…

It had all started a few years before. My husband, Rob, and I were both professionals. He was a computer programmer, and I was a composer and music teacher. We enjoyed our jobs and were good at them, but we wanted to be financially independent.

We had done all the things: property investing courses, options trading seminars, read Robert Kiyosaki's books and attended Tony Robbins' seminars.

We hadn't only learnt; we'd built a portfolio of four properties, dabbled in stock and options trading, and had invested in shares. The properties were growing strongly, but we had reached our borrowing limit, and we were impatient. Building a business with cashflow seemed to be the answer to being able to invest more.

I had also started and closed my first business—a music education consultancy running workshops to teach high school music students how to perform confidently on stage.

I knew nothing about business when I started, but I had learned a lot about how to create and market products people wanted to buy. I was even doing content marketing before it was a thing by writing and sending out photocopied newsletters every term to all the music teachers in the state, telling them about my successful workshops.

Every time I sent the newsletter, teachers would call me to enquire, and I sold them on the phone pretty much by assuming they wanted to book. I didn't know any differently! Somehow, I never figured out that if I wanted more bookings, I should send out the newsletter more often.

After a while, however, I did realise that the business was totally dependent on my time. I had built a fun job for myself, but I wanted to leverage both my time and income from it. I was looking for ways to achieve this, but Rob suggested that if I were going to put in that effort, I should look for a bigger opportunity, so we had our eyes open for something new.

Our first child had been born two years earlier, and we wanted a business that would allow Rob to be around more rather than working such long hours and being on call 24/7.

We also felt there was something more for us, and business was a great vehicle to have an impact, make some money, and be a resource to fund causes that were close to our hearts.

We wanted to be able to create change and freedom, both for ourselves and others.

As we were searching for business opportunities, we came across a guru who was teaching how to buy a business that had potential but was underperforming, renovate it, and then resell it for profit. It made sense, and we thought, *How hard could it be? We're smart. We can do this.*

We sold our house to free up some equity and started looking through the papers for businesses to buy. We came across one that seemed a great fit for our skills: Aussie Mushrooms. It was the franchisorship for a work-at-home opportunity. The business sold franchises to people to grow mushrooms at home. The franchisor made money by selling the mushrooms at the wholesale markets as well as selling franchises. We thought it was a good fit for our skills in training, marketing, and logistics.

We met with Graham Faker (name changed to protect the guilty), one of two partners, and started negotiating. He even offered to become our business partner, keeping his half of the business, which seemed like a good idea since he had the expertise.

We took our time to investigate the opportunity. We asked for documents, Rob visited suppliers, and I put together financial projections based on the info we gathered. We even talked to a mushroom growing expert.

It looked good to us, so we got our lawyers to draw up the paperwork, signed the documents, and finally had our own business.

It was only two days later when Rob visited our best franchisee that everything started to unravel. He came home and said to me, "These people are doing everything right. You should see their setup and the amount of effort they have put in. But they can't grow enough mushrooms to make this viable."

My heart sank.

And then the phone calls started. The franchisees found out that the business had new owners and our phone started to ring constantly with franchisees complaining that they had been sold a scam and demanding their money back.

What could we say to them? We had no answers, no money to pay them, and they were angry—rightly so. It got so bad that we had to leave our phone off the hook permanently.

I remember standing in the kitchen with our friend, Hunter, thinking, "What are we going to do?" Our dream was crashing around our ears in a big way. Hunter said to us, "Two days ago, I was so jealous that you guys had found a great opportunity, but now I'm so glad I am not you."

We felt numb and dazed. The more we dug into what had happened, the more we realised how badly we had been had. We found out that Graham Faker was a professional conman and had actually been jailed for fraud before by ASIC, Australia's corporate regulatory body. He had lied to us, faked documents, set up an elaborate scam, and then sold it to us. We had been thoroughly scammed!

In the end, the only thing to do seemed to be to get a court order to freeze his bank account to protect the money we had paid.

Our lawyers really should have advised us to cut our losses, both because they had no expertise in conducting cases in the Supreme Court and because that action started an extremely stressful and costly six-month court case that ended in the mediation session I described at the start of this chapter.

We got a fraction of our money back and lost two properties in the process, so it was financially devastating for us.

We felt very stupid. We considered ourselves to be smart professionals, and here we were, duped by a conman.

As I thought about what had happened, I realised that we had no idea how to do due diligence properly. We thought we had done the right things, but we really had no idea how to assess the potential of this opportunity.

I decided I was going to get really good at assessing business opportunities so this could never happen to us again.

And I had a plan to make this happen.

Now, years later, I realise there was another factor at play in our downfall.

I was avoiding fear. Fear of negotiation, fear of being seen as too pushy, fear of being judged. We didn't get out hands dirty enough in the due diligence process.

We didn't dig and test assumptions. We hadn't asked the right questions and so hadn't tested the right things. We were hoping this business would work rather than being absolutely sure it would. And that was a fatal assumption.

My new plan was to go to Uni and learn how to assess opportunities and build great businesses.

I come from a family of teachers. I obviously wasn't good at business, but I knew I was good at learning. If I could learn what I needed to know to spot and shape a great business opportunity, then I believed I could be successful. It was a lack of knowledge that had tripped us up, not anything to do with our abilities.

I enrolled in a Masters of Entrepreneurship and Innovation program. In fact, I came into it with a new business venture to assess.

I had been offered an opportunity to be the Australian agent for an outsourcing firm in India. I wanted to provide a service that allowed accountants to outsource their low-ticket work and use their in-house staff on higher-value work instead. It seemed feasible since outsourcing was just taking off and there was a shortage of accountants in Australia.

I gathered a great team of other masters students, and we started assessing my new opportunity using what we were learning in our degree. I started to fall in love with this process of assessing and tweaking ideas until I knew for sure whether they would work or not.

Long story short, about three months in, I found some information on my competitors that listed how many clients they each had. When I looked at that info, I knew that I could never build this business to the revenue goals I had set. It wasn't a big enough opportunity. In truth, I was probably too early with this one. Three to five years later, it could have become the business I had imagined.

I ditched that business.

But the great thing was, it had only taken me three months of part-time work and zero dollars to find out that it was not viable.

After that, I did everything I could to master the science and art of assessing startup ideas and launching in low-risk ways with a minimum of time and money.

I entered and won local, national, and international business plan competitions.

I co-founded my own startups and wrote about starting up on my blog, *Ready Set Startup*.

I lectured in entrepreneurship.

I advised and coached tech startups on strategies and pitching and wrote business plans for them.

I became obsessed about cracking the code on what it takes to tip the scales in favour of success for startup founders.

But in everything I did, I noticed that I, and other women, kept hitting the same wall.

When I enrolled for my Masters in Entrepreneurship, I had to attend an interview before being accepted into the course. I sat down, and almost the first thing the admissions officer said to me was, "Why have you applied to this course? Why don't you do a business certificate at TAFE instead What's makes you think you can cope in this course? The guys in this course are alpha males and can be very aggressive. It's competitive."

I was dumbfounded. She was questioning my ability to be an entrepreneur because of my appearance, because I was a woman.

In fact, I blitzed the course and worked well with some of the most alpha of the males in the course. Many of them wanted to work with me because I was smart, and I got stuff done.

Another time, I attended a meetup about applying for a local accelerator. I was standing next to a woman who was an expert in her field. But as we listened and male speaker after male speaker came to the stage, she came to the conclusion that this wasn't for her. It broke my heart because I knew she had a great idea and that this accelerator could help her, but she was feeling excluded because she was a woman in a male-dominated space.

As I watched more and more support develop for startup founders, I realised very little of it was accessible to me or other women.

After numerous experiences like this, I came to the conclusion that I and other women founders needed a different kind of support and mentoring than what is currently available because the status quo is not working for us.

I really believe that women have unique and important startup ideas that the world needs, and those ideas deserve the same support and help that is available to male-founded startups.

When I looked at following the traditional path of getting investor funding for my startup, I was shocked to learn that only 0.9% of businesses get venture funding and only 2.2% of that goes to female-founded startups. Yet, this was touted as the path to follow.

There was no way I was going to play a game where the odds were stacked against me. I wanted to play my own game; one I could win!

I started looking for alternative ways to start up with minimal upfront money and the quickest possible time to getting revenue in the door.

What I found as I implemented this focus with the founders I was coaching was that for almost every idea, there is a way to launch and get revenue in the door sooner rather than later. It doesn't matter if it's an app, a platform, physical products, services, or anything else. I also found that when we used some entrepreneurial strategies, most founders need a lot less money to start up than they think.

That means you get to keep *all* of your business. You're not waiting on anyone else to give your startup the tick of approval to launch.

The key to this, though, is understanding that starting up is not a linear path. It's much more like a jigsaw and you probably already have most of the pieces.

Your most important job as a founder at the beginning of your startup is to find the perfect fit between your customers, your product or service, the market and yourself as a founder.

I designed a process to get the information about those four pieces, quickly find out what was missing, and then use simple ways to get that missing information from the market.

The great thing about this process is that by doing it, you actually launch your business as you go by taking low-risk actions as well as responding and changing to cater for market feedback. That means you are creating a startup that is super attractive to your customers and that they will pay for.

I realised I needed to be prepared to put myself out there and go against the standard thinking on startups and share this process of building a startup from revenue rather than funding because women need it to get their startups off the ground.

I created LaunchLab, a completely different accelerator model that takes female founders through this process so they can take focused action, launch their startups, and get revenue and paying customers.

I don't want anyone else to go through the experience I had of hoping their business will work and not knowing how to find out for sure, potentially wasting a lot of time and being thousands of dollars out of pocket. I want to give them the tools to build a robust startup that will be life-changing for them, their families, and the world.

Because the world needs more female-founded startups.

Business has forced me to face every insecurity and flaw I have.

This journey has given me a lot of belief in myself. I've become okay with putting myself out there and pushing through my fears.

And even though it was so painful at the time, I am glad that we experienced being scammed so badly and losing so much money. If that had not happened, I would not have gone on this journey or learnt what it takes to create a successful startup. And that journey has led me to a business that I love and am deeply passionate about.

I am forging my own way, and I'm helping other women to forge their own way, too, using entrepreneurship to create a better world.

And I really couldn't think of anything else I would rather do.

ABOUT SUSAN JONES

Susan Jones is an entrepreneur, startup advisor and coach, and the founder of ReadySetStartup.com.

Knowing how hard it is at the very early stages of your business, Susan focuses on showing entrepreneurs how to find great ideas, test them in the market, plan and strategize to launch successfully and quickly, and then work out how you can fund the whole thing. Her superpower is creating strategies to avoid early investment and get to profitability sooner rather than later.

She has lectured on entrepreneurship for the past ten years alongside running her own businesses and mothering two kids, and she has a host of frameworks and strategies for startup success at her fingertips.

Susan is currently creating a more democratized and inclusive—but still highly effective—accelerator and funding model for female founders of tech and tech enabled startups.

And as a reward for reading this far, Susan has created a special bonus for readers of this book. You can find it at
www.readysetstartup.com/overcoming-adversity-readers

THE SOLDIER'S WAY

by Nathan Kay

Henry Ford once said, *"If you think you can, you will. But if you think you cannot, then you are absolutely right!"*

As a child, I was always sick and hurt from one thing or another. I was wild and crazy. I spent my youth doing all the things that little boys should do and many things they should not do. I climbed trees, ran around in the woods, played sports, started fires, and got into trouble at any expense, but most importantly, I learned from my mistakes along the way. No matter what I faced, it never stopped me. It never slowed me down. It only added fuel to the fire inside of me that made me want to accomplish my goals even more. The inner child runs wild and fuels the fire of my adult self.

When I was little, the curiosity inside of me kept me and my brothers in trouble; the adventures never stopped. We were always into something, and that usually meant something that would get us into trouble. I'm sure we aged our parents significantly because of our shenanigans. I spent more time in the hospital as a child than most people should ever have to. I had childhood epilepsy and asthma. I fell out of a tree and bruised my kidneys. I had Lyme disease and Rocky Mountain spotted fever. A doctor overdosed me with pain medications, which shut down my digestive track, almost killing me. One day, while I was riding my bike, I was hit by a sixteen-year-old little rich girl who was drinking and driving in her daddy's BMW. The list goes on and on.

The most tragic event was being hit by the girl while driving drunk. I laid there, clinically dead on the asphalt, in the one-hundred-degree Georgia heat until someone came to save me.

177

The event left me in a horrible state. I had third-degree burns on my left arm, my ear was just about torn off, and I spent months afterward in a wheelchair. The doctors said I would never walk again. The event was horrible, although I do not remember a lot from this period as I incurred severe head trauma. Memory issues still bother me to this day.

Through all of this, I knew inside that I was not going to let what happened to me stop me. I knew more than anything that I wanted to be a soldier. I was that child that looked at guys in uniform and knew that I would be among them one day. My medical conditions were not going to stop me. The more people told me that I couldn't or wouldn't be able to do something, the more I would tell myself, "I am going to do it!"

I knew as a child that I was going to serve in the military. I knew that I would have to get it for myself. No one was going to do it for me. Everyone could say they supported me, but that only went so far. My goals were always at the front of my mind. I knew that my mental strength would be the deciding factor in getting what I wanted and how I wanted to get there. So, I looked deep inside and told myself never to stop. Never quit. Never give up.

In my teen years, I started down a dark path of drugs, drinking, and fighting. I lost two people who I grew up with who had a bigger impact on me than I realized at the time. The year I turned sixteen, I lost more friends and family than I ever wanted to count. It seemed like I was at a funeral every other weekend. I spiraled out of control and quickly lost focus of what I wanted to do in life. I was in trouble with the law, no longer in high school, and self-medicated most of the time.

At seventeen years old, I knew that I had to change things and get back on track to where I wanted to be. I started the process of joining the military and was relentless with the recruiters. At the time, I was in trouble with the law, did not have a job, and had dropped out of high school. None of the branches wanted me. For months, I kept visiting them, and for months, they all turned me away. Then one day, a Navy recruiter said he would try to help me. He told me I was a persistent guy and saw that I was serious. He took me in back and made me take a drug test and a practice ASVAB (this is a test of basic skills to join the military and qualify for your job). I passed my drug test and scored well on the test.

He told me I could do pretty much whatever I wanted in the military. For the next six months, I was back and forth, and they kept turning me away. I got a job working construction in Atlanta. I thought getting in the military was a lost cause but then I got the call. They wanted to see me. I went into the Military Entrance Processing Center, did another interview, and signed some paperwork. They told me to pack my bags because I was leaving the next day. On March 28, 2000, I left for Navy basic training. My dream was coming true!

Along came 9/11. I was working on the flight deck of the U.S.S. *John F. Kennedy*. We were set to go to sea that day for a training exercise. Within an hour of the second plane hitting the towers, we were at sea, and fighter jets were landing. What was happening? I was nineteen at the time and knew my job, but I had no clue what was going on. For the next forty-eight days, we were in the middle of the Atlantic Ocean. I was lost and confused once again.

In January, my best friend, Bryan, killed himself one night while I was working. Once again, I had lost someone very dear to me. I had once again been shaken to my core. His death left so many things unanswered. In the year and a half that we knew each other, we had become best friends—brothers. On the way to his funeral, I stopped in Atlanta to see an old friend. In all the emotional turmoil and craziness of it all, we went and got married the day before Bryan's funeral. It was a bad time, as a month later, I was leaving on a deployment to the Middle East. It was seven-and-a-half months in the Middle East before I would return to my family and friends. I was alone and isolated. I once again started down a path of self-destruction that involved lots of drinking. By the time I returned to the states, I was drinking a bottle of whiskey a day. The next few years were a blur and not fulfilling at all, so I left the Navy and explored civilian life.

Shortly after leaving the Navy, fate would show her ugly face once again and strike me with the biggest blow of my life. My brother, Mike, had died at twenty-six years old. He killed himself while I was on a weekend getaway to Brazil. I had only been gone for the weekend, but upon landing in Miami, I turned on my phone and had over thirty voice mails. I didn't listen to any of them; I just called my mom and found out what happened. By that point in my life, my family had come to rely on me for my mental strength. I was the one that everyone looked to when it came to trouble or problems. They looked to me to handle the situation and plan his funeral. And I did. I was the shoulder that everyone cried on, and the one that made the decisions on the funeral. I was the one who took the calls and the one who had to inform my grandmother. But no one was there for me. Down the rabbit hole I went, and my family sat in wonder as I once again embarked on my adventures around the world.

The next year was anything but normal for me. I was going to flight school, waiting tables for money, drinking heavily, and rambling around the country and world. I got a divorce and moved constantly. Then I met Kristen. Our relationship starting out was anything but normal as she caught me at a time when I was still spiraling out of control. She held on for dear life, just as she continues to hold on as my wife.

Let me pause to say that Kristen is my wife, my best friend, and my greatest supporter. She is the mother of my children and the reason that I am the person I am today. Our relationship is not perfect, but it is special. She stands by with all my craziness and supports me through all of it. And believe me, there is a lot of craziness! She has gone with me to every corner of the globe that my military and civilian career has taken us, and she continues to take care of me. She has stood by and even slept in my hospital bed with me during times of need. She keeps me in check and balanced. She takes care of us. I do everything for her and our children. She is my rock. She is my lobster.

In the summer of 2007, I returned to the military—this time in the Army. The Army is what I had always wanted. I didn't fit in with the people in the Navy. I had a different mentality. The Army was more my style. Kristen and I were married shortly thereafter, and off to Germany we went. Our first child, Dessi, arrived in May of 2008. Boy, did my world change forever. She is my mini-me for sure. It was a true turning point in my life. I finally started to grow up and pull my head out of my ass.

I was sent to Iraq later that year, and things took a turn once again. Fast forward to November 2010, and we welcomed our second child, Brince. He is my little dude for sure—a typical rough and tough little boy. The Army still had plans, though, and it wasn't long before they sent me to Afghanistan. The next few years we moved repeatedly with the Army. I was deployed yet again, but something was still missing. Something inside of me just wasn't right. I wanted to be more. I wanted to be a husband, a father, an entrepreneur, and a soldier. But not just a soldier, I wanted to be an officer and command soldiers. I wanted to be a role model for my family—not just an entrepreneur but also a mentor.

On December 31, 2017, I separated from the active Army and joined the National Guard so I could become a commissioned officer, which I did in March of 2019. I bought a bread delivery company and was very ambitious. I knew with my work and desire to learn that I could turn this thing into something great. At the time of purchase, it was doing roughly $60,000 a year. Within seven months, I had more than doubled that. I went from working with four stores to eight. I was going after everything that I could to grow it and make a good run of it. I was trying to find people to work for me and could not find someone to stick with it. It was easy to grow, but the hard, physical work took its toll on my body. I woke up in the middle of the night, worked long hours, and never got to see my family. I even broke my ankle at work one day. I took a day off for surgery and was back at work the next day.

Then when I thought things were going to really start to pick up for me, in walked corporate America and punched me in the face. Hard! One of the big box stores that I worked with decided to change things up, and my business that was making good money at the time went to less than $26,000 a year in a few weeks. There was nothing I could do about it. I was working just as hard to keep it going but getting nowhere. I was begging store managers for help, but there was nothing they could do. The harder I worked, the less it paid off, and I eventually had to file for bankruptcy. I went down the rabbit hole once again and started in on my depression and drinking. Kristen brought me back, though. She would not let me run away and hide. So, I picked myself up and said to myself, "Stop being a bitch" and got after it.

I can't be stopped! Someone once told me, "Fail often, fail fast, and fail forward." My life has been full of many failures along the way. I have learned from all of them, and I don't see any of them as a real failure but more so a learning experience. Now I help others and guide them down the right path.

I used my network and landed a job as a government contractor to pay the bills and get back on my feet. I knew that this time would be different. I was going to take advantage of my education and change directions. I was going to help others get started. I was going to help them get on the right path. I was going to get back to my roots and to what I truly knew—how to train, lead, and motivate. That was it! Working with veterans is what I needed to do. So, Un-Deployed was born in December 2018.

I started Un-Deployed to help veterans who, like myself, wanted more; veterans who wanted to be entrepreneurs but didn't know how to get started. They knew they still had something to offer the world, but they were not sure exactly how or what to do. I would help them find employment, careers, and position them for success no matter what. I was and always have been a leader. People look to me for guidance and advice. People have always felt like they could talk to me because they knew I would help them. So, why not take these skills and put them to good use? I have over twenty years of experience with leadership in the military, corporate America, and as an entrepreneur.

I have taken it a step farther, though. I wanted to truly change someone's life for the better. For that reason, I decided to start a coaching program and mentor veterans. People need help with getting past themselves and drowning out the noise to kick some ass and accomplish greatness. Sometimes, we just need someone to point us in the right direction, someone to give us that kick in the ass.

You see, no one talks to you more than you, so start telling yourself that you can, and you will! Start telling yourself that you are ready for greatness. Start putting things into the context that you need to accomplish your goals. Stop saying I will and start saying I am. Start wanting more. Start achieving more. Start demanding more of yourself. It's your life and your goals. No one is going to do it for you. Ignore all the noise around you and get busy. Write down your goals and publicly address them with the world. Tell all your friends and family what you're doing. Then put your head down and get to work. Stop being a bitch and be a warrior! Be a savage! Be a soldier! Be a fighter! Be the person you always dreamed of being!

Train, lead, and motivate!
That is what I know, and that is what I do!
Do you know how to launch your product?
Do you need help figuring out a course of action?
Are you looking to build a brand?
What are you doing to position yourself as an authority in your niche?
STOP BEING A BITCH!

ABOUT NATHAN KAY

I am just an average man; plain and simple, born and raised in the small town of Swainsboro, Georgia. No matter what I have done in my life, I acknowledge that nothing is more important than being a husband and father. I have served in the U.S. Military since March of 2000. I have had several deployments to Iraq and Afghanistan. I have owned a couple of different companies and helped others launch theirs. I have known success and I have fallen. I don't believe that anything is a failure, just a learning experience on your path to success. I have traveled the world, and I serve others above myself. I want that to be my legacy. I hope my chapter is a source of fuel for your soul! Let it serve as an inspiration to drive you to take the next step in your life!

TAKE ACTION TODAY AND FOLLOW THE LINK BELOW!
www.bizvetsolutions.com

OVERCOMING ADVERSITY: BODY, MIND, AND HEART

by Jennifer Silverston

"Maintain a spiritual practice;
even if you don't get enlightened in this lifetime, you'll get lit up.
As they say, practice makes perfect.
Or even better, practice is perfect."

—Lama Surya Das;
Awakening to the Sacred: Creating A Spiritual Life from Scratch

Overcoming adversity takes persistence, determination, and calculated action.

Adversity doesn't end; all we can control is our mindset and our reaction.

Why do I believe these things? Because I have faced adversity in my health—many times.

Which has led me to become a student of life in how to heal, how to fail, and how to succeed.

We all need a pity party sometimes. Go ahead and have it. Take twenty minutes, or an hour, or even a day if you need it. Really cry or mope or be angry and scream. We need to allow ourselves to feel those upset feelings when we are facing adversity.

Just don't stay there too long.

In 2002, I could barely walk. I had been in a boat accident while working for the National Park Service and had a severe spinal injury. I was twenty-two. My pity party was huge. My life as I knew it had ended, and I was swirling in a deep pool of pain and uncertainty.

Because of my age and the extent of my injuries, my doctor put me on a ten-year healing plan. To a twenty-two-year-old, that was pretty much inconceivable.

I was receiving all the best medical care that Western medicine had to offer and was in a wait-and-see phase for years. How much would I recover?

I remember I would wake up in the morning, and someone in my family would have put out a little glass of milk and crackers on my bedside table. I would wake up and take the pain meds with a little sustenance and go back to sleep.

I could not be awake in my own body.

There was a desk and a computer next to my bed. I couldn't go far, but I could get myself over there. Somehow, I got involved with an online group tutorial studying the book *Awakening to the Sacred* by Lama Surya Das.

Reading that book was pure inspiration. Every word was like a breath of fresh air.

I realized there was more to my healing than what Western medicine could offer. I continued to do my physical therapy and Western medicine, but I also began dabbling.

I dabbled in massages, acupuncture, yoga, smells, essential oil blends, and topical salves. Anything that would make my experience even a little bit better got added to my Wellness Toolkit.

A rock I could hold in my hand. Wearing bright colors. Playing happy and beautiful music. Full-spectrum lights. All of it. Give me all of it. I was open to anything that would help me feel better.

Persistence. Determination. Calculated action.

What did I learn? When something works, repeat it. Over and over.

When something doesn't work, increases pain, or leaves you feeling down, avoid it.

There is a key in there: Take note of what makes your situation better and what makes it worse. Do the things that make it better and avoid or minimize what makes it worse.

Sounds simple, but it takes doing. And it takes some deep honesty with yourself.

Seven years later, I had improved but was still not normal. I couldn't drive or work like a normal person. I was still in a lot of pain. Still in physical therapy.

A Chinese kung fu master came to my small town as a Fulbright Scholar for the university. I went to a free workshop he offered and was amazed. I could do the exercises, and they made me feel a little bit better.

By now, you probably know me well enough to know what I did next. I enrolled in the university so I could take Master Han's class: Traditional Chinese Martial Arts. I needed to learn more.

Soon, I was obsessed. The movements were easy and fun, and they made me feel a little bit better each time I did them.

After a few months, each of my three physical therapists commented, "Are you doing something different? The physical therapy seems to be working better." I told them I was doing something like tai chi and they all said, "Oh, we've read about that. It is supposed to be very good for rehabilitation."

Why didn't anyone tell me that before? Like seven years ago?

The time was now.

Persistance. Determination. Calculated action.

I trained every day. For years. To this day, actually. I am still doing those same exercises, and they still make me feel a little bit (or a lot) better every single time.

I was always calling my friends and asking them to come practice with me until one friend said, "Jen, you are so good at this, maybe you should do this as a teacher."

Hmmm, perhaps Kora was right. Then I could earn money while healing myself and helping others heal themselves as well. I trained to become a teacher and started formally teaching in 2008.

Thank goodness, I gradually got a little better and a little better and a little better.

It took a really long time.

And that is one of the true keys, I believe: small gains over a long span of time.

In healing, in business, even in relationships. It is a slow piling of small gains, almost imperceptible at times.

And that is where faith comes in, believing in a better version of yourself or situation for the future. That dream can add a lot of fuel to your tank.

I believed I could heal. I believed I could succeed. But let me take you even a little deeper than that. There was *no way* I was accepting my condition as it was.

I refused. I could not believe that this was the way my life would stay.

And so I took action. Calculated action. Again and again.

I developed a chalkboard checklist of my back exercises. I wrote lists of exercises and put them up on huge dance mirrors.

Every time I walked past the mirror, my notes and my posture and the sight of myself would remind me to *do your exercises*.

I used a bell timer to keep me progressing through the exercises.

Physical therapy is like poking at your weakest, most painful parts.

Once I learned qi gong, kung fu, and tai chi, those modalities helped with all the rest. They helped relax my tense shoulders, taught me how to breathe again after holding my breath through so much pain. These ancient mind-body practices help soothe the nervous system and soften strong emotions.

The combination of the laser focus of Western medicine plus the whole body tonic of Eastern medicine was a winning combination.

It seemed like it took forever, but sometimes you just have to trust the process. There was a long time where nothing seemed to be improving. Like a really long time. Like years.

In that time, you are acting on belief, on hope, and on that future vision you hold.

And perhaps that was why I was drawn to the invisible world. Spirituality is belief in the unseen. And like Lama Surya Das says, "Even if you don't get enlightened in this lifetime, you'll get lit up by the practice."

Every time I got those checkmarks on the chalkboard, I had a sense of accomplishment. Every time I made it to the end bell on my timer, another accomplishment.

I could celebrate those small wins day by day while I was waiting for the big results to start appearing.

In those situations of adversity, do the practice. Go through the motions of the things you know will get you those small gains. Go through the motions even when you are not feeling like it.

I used to repeat this mantra, "I am completely healed, and it feels amazing."

For a long time, it was so far from my reality that it was cryable.

But I kept repeating it. Imagining myself feeling powerful and free.

Years later, I feel pretty amazing.

I notice that sometimes I am doing the tai chi, and sometimes the tai chi carries me through the practice. Either way, I feel better in the end.

So, find that. Whatever it is for you.

I know tai chi and meditation really help me. Affirmations. Singing with my friends. Also walks in nature or looking at flowers. These things help me feel better every time.

Find out what really helps you.

Repeat again and again.

I surrounded myself with powerful healers, mentors, and people I could turn to who could help me along my road.

That is another key. Have guidance. Find someone who has seen this sort of thing before and can help you steady the course.

I used to look at trees bent or growing on rock ledges, and I would think, *I am made of the same stuff.*

You, too, are made of the same stuff.

Your body has incredible wisdom, an incredible power to heal. Our minds are so powerful they can make our world beautiful or harsh, no matter what the external circumstances.

As an entrepreneur, your state of mind has a huge influence on the work you produce.

Your mind state and your body state can influence your business.

And they can influence each other. We know when the stress is high, the shoulders go up. We know when the body hurts, it stresses the mind.

Use that relationship to your advantage. Use the mind to relax the body. Meditation. Intention. Affirmation. You can use the body to relax the mind.

When dealing with adversity in business or health or life in general, remember that in each situation, there is both danger and opportunity.

I understand the overwhelm, but the more we can hold ourselves in a state of calm power, the more the answers will reveal themselves. Find lessons in the adversity and put them to use in your growth.

You always have time to take care of the vehicle of your body.

You always have time to take care of your mind.

This looks different for each person, but there are many ways both ancient and modern that can help enhance our wellness and our power. Do them regularly.

A practice, a ritual of wellness, helps stabilize us through the storms of life.

Overcoming adversity takes persistence, determination, and calculated action.

When you apply the right strategies, you truly can achieve anything.

ABOUT JENNIFER SILVERSTON

Jennifer has a degree in marine biology from Boston University and worked for the National Park Service on an endangered species project. While working, she sustained a severe spinal injury that sidelined her for years. By combining Western medicine and Eastern practices, she was able to rebuild her body and her life.

Jennifer has studied with some of today's greatest transformational and mind-body practice leaders including Master Jingshen Han of Zhuhai, China, Dr. Roger Jahnke, Dr. Paul Lam, Dr. Maria Formolo, Dr. Renxin Yang, Donna Eden, Jack Canfield, and Marie Diamond.

Jennifer taught tai chi and qi gong at Northern Michigan University for years before starting her own business in 2015 called Tai Chi with Jennifer. She has since taught public classes in communities all over the United States and even internationally. She co-led over thirty backwoods retreats, "Between the Mountain & the Stream," and has assisted in training other tai chi and qi gong instructors.

More recently, she has been dabbling in technology to reach even more people. Since October, she has taught over 150 online tai chi classes. Jennifer's vision to help others heal themselves is inspired by her own healing journey.

To participate in Jennifer's Online Tai Chi Programs, sign up at
taichiwithjennifer.com

You can connect with Jennifer on Facebook for more inspiring stories and latest updates at
www.facebook.com/jennifer.silverston

BELIEVE IN YOU

by Rebecca Chadburn

*"Life isn't about waiting for the storm to pass;
it's about learning how to dance in the rain."*

F inancial freedom has always been important to me, and I decided early on that I was willing to live like most people won't so that in the future, I can live like most people can't. At age 19, I married my high school sweetheart. By age 24, we had bought our first house and had two kids. I enjoyed life as a stay-at-home mom and supportive wife while my husband worked and went to school. We lived on a fairly tight budget to stay out of debt and build our savings.

We soon discovered the income from my husband's warehouse job wasn't enough, so I found a job I could do from home. I worked while the kids napped or when they went to bed at night. It was tough, but we really wanted the money it provided. In addition to working, I read all kinds of books on investing, money-saving tips, and wealth building. Not only did I read the books, but I implemented the strategies I learned. While my husband was off at college, I was learning at home.

One night in 2000, I was lying in bed waiting for my husband to come home from school. The kids were asleep, and I was enjoying some quiet time to myself. He arrived late and quietly walked into our bedroom. I could tell something was off. When I asked what was going on, he looked down at his feet and quietly confessed that he needed to clear his conscious. He let me know that he had been cheating on me—for the past five years. I was stunned. I didn't know what to do. All sorts of thoughts raced through my mind, but I was speechless.

I came from a divorced family and knew divorce was not something I wanted. I watched my mom struggle emotionally and financially for years. I knew that I did not want to follow in her footsteps. So, I took a few weeks to process things in my head, and after much discussion, we chose to stay together. I was humiliated about the affairs, so I never told anyone what was going on in my life, and I suffered silently.

The next eleven years were a rollercoaster, not only in our relationship but also in my head. I never felt that I was good enough for anything. I didn't believe in myself, and I lived in constant fear. My anxiety was through the roof. I was ashamed that my husband had cheated on me. I was also concerned about being naive and having it happen again. I began to question life and what was going on around me constantly.

On top of that, I often wondered what was wrong with me. Why was he cheating on me? I put a whole new level of pressure on myself. I began to believe that the only way he wouldn't cheat on me again was if I kept a clean house, provided nice meals, was physically fit, and had successful kids. I threw my heart and soul into being the "perfect" wife and mom.

We eventually had two more children, and I was content staying at home and supporting his career. However, I began to feel undervalued, and my self-esteem was at an all-time low. I was exhausted from trying to be super wife. I eventually thought that making some money of my own would help me feel better about myself. I also wanted to have some of my own money so I didn't feel completely dependent on my husband. And let's be honest, there was always this little voice in the back of my head telling myself that one day I might have to provide for myself and my kids financially.

To fill this void, I started looking for something to do from home again. Lucky for me, I had a friend who was looking for an assistant in his real estate business that was booming during the crash of 2008. He was a listing agent with a couple of banks and needed someone to process all the offers. This was a fantastic fit for me and taught me a lot about real estate. I was able to see all these investors snatching up properties right and left. It was my responsibility to process the transaction from beginning to end. I learned what investors looked for, how they created their offer, and how the transaction was completed. After a couple of months, I knew that I wanted in on a deal. I understood and could see the real value in purchasing buy-and-hold properties and the financial freedom it could provide.

Fortunately, my agent brought a deal into the office that I felt I could do. It was a property that already had tenants in it, and we were listing it as a short sale. I put an offer in with the bank and then waited. Short sales can often take months or years to complete, but I was willing to wait. Each day, I would call the bank for a status update, and each day, I was told there was no decision on the offer. Then, one afternoon, during my inquiry, I was told the property was going to the county auction in two days. I had no idea how an auction worked, but I knew we were showing up to bid on that property. Luckily for us, other investors didn't have time to really investigate the property, and we were the only bidders, so we walked away with the deal. It was a great investment, and I was super pumped about the whole thing. I finally felt like I was capable and valuable. It was so rewarding to finally put the knowledge I had acquired to good use.

A couple years later, my husband came home from work, sat me down in the office, and said he didn't have the "moral compass" I needed him to have. Turns out there were more affairs. That was it; I was done. I was no longer going to take ownership of his choices. I was not going to keep beating myself down because of how I felt when I was with him, and I realized I wasn't doing my kids any favors by staying married. I was done lying to myself and everyone around me. We divorced, and I walked away from the very financially comfortable life I was used to.

Even though I knew it was the right thing to do, I was terrified. I soon realized I had stayed in that relationship way too long because I wasn't sure of myself. Because of my self-doubt, I didn't know how I was going to take care of myself and my four kids without him. Upon leaving the relationship, I knew I needed to make a plan. I needed to regain control of my life.

At the time I divorced, I didn't have a college education or an established career. I had been a stay-at-home mom and supported my ex-husband while he built his career. So, I did what I thought any new single mom would do. I went back to school. I received my degree in psychology with a minor in business. I can't say the degree has been super helpful, but it was something I wanted for myself, and I am glad that I was able to earn it. The challenging thing was that, after graduating, I still didn't know how I was going to financially provide for myself, especially once child support and alimony ended.

Even though the divorce was a shock to all my family and friends, they were very supportive and helpful. My kids and I ended up moving near family, and piece by piece, I began to put my life back together. While my focus was on being a good mom, I was still on my quest for financial freedom. In fact, getting divorced increased the fire inside of me. I was now solely responsible, and I felt like I had something to prove.

One of the first steps I took in my pursuit for financial freedom was to create a plan. I took some time, sat down, and looked at where I wanted to be. I outlined all of my expenses and determined how much money I would need to produce in order to live the life I wanted. Next, I looked at all the ways I could create income. I quickly realized that the only way I was going to be able to produce the kind of income I wanted was to continue to invest in real estate. The problem was that I needed money to do so. I knew I didn't want to work a 9-to-5, but I was willing to live like most people won't so that in the future I could live like most people can't, and I found a job. Having the additional income from my job has allowed me to purchase, as of the writing of this book, six income properties. The monthly cash flow I receive from my rentals exceeds the income I initially set out to create when I got divorced.

After doing this for the past ten years, I have discovered you don't need to know everything in the beginning. Systems create wealth, anybody can be successful in real estate investing, and to change your life, you need to take action. One of the best things about real estate is that it is never going away. There has never been a better time in history for you to step up and do your own thing. With buy-and-hold properties, you can do your own thing in an industry that is future-proof.

Here are four tips I have for anyone looking to change their financial future through real estate investing:

1. Find a mentor. Search for a real estate investing coach or individual who has already achieved the level of success that you want to have. This will shorten your learning curve by leveraging someone else's knowledge, mistakes, and experience.
2. Understand financing options. There are ways to get started without money, but the reality is that you will more than likely need to access financing at some point. It is always smart to be aware of the financing strategies used throughout the industry. Some programs to learn about are no-money-down loans, creative financing, lease options, hard money loans, and more.
3. Do your research. Figure out what type of strategy you want to use for your investments. Some options are wholesaling, fix-and-flip, buy-and-hold, or commercial real estate. Determine which strategy will best suit you.
4. Build relationships. The team I have built has been a huge factor in my success. Having realtors, lenders, title officers, and property managers on board takes the stress out of each transaction.

It is only through a lot of hard work, a ton of time, some serious heartache, and good mentors that I have been able to get to the point I am today. I am finally confident in myself. I feel valuable and accepting of myself. I believe in my abilities, and

I can finally chase after my dreams. I am currently married to a wonderful man who has joined me on my journey and is very supportive in my endeavors. Together, we have seven children we encourage to be financially independent. It is my mission to bring hope and guidance to those who want to regain control of their life and financial future.

If I could show you the steps to take you from being financially unhappy to happy, would that change your life? Do you want to live the life you have dreamed of? Would you like to speed up the process of retirement? Do you want more money? Do you want more control over your life? If you answered yes to these questions, I would love to connect.

ABOUT REBECCA CHADBURN

Rebecca was born and raised in Salt Lake City, UT, and currently resides in southern Utah. She and her husband, Jeremy, have seven children and a handful of grandchildren. Rebecca has a bachelor's degree in psychology and a minor in business. She is also a certified health coach. After building her seven-figure real estate portfolio, she decided to start her own business. You can find Rebecca riding her bike on the beach, hiking in the mountains, or enjoying time with her family on the lake. Rebecca is passionate about health, wellness, and financial empowerment and wants to help others reach their full potential. Her motto is, "Decisions determine your destiny."

If you would like to connect with me I can be found at facebook.com/believeinrebeccachadburn

F*@$ ADVERSITY

by Jon Vaughn

Write to you.
Speak to you.
Capture You.
Inspire you.
Inspire myself.

F*@$ adversity. Those are my goals. Aspiring to these goals is already difficult considering the very definition of the word "adversity," and the fact that we have all had our relative adverse little experiences and perspectives in life.

Watching my father beat my sister almost to death for getting drugged and raped may seem adverse to some people, but to others, it may be a fond and familiar feeling.

Dictionary

Search for a word   Q

🔊 **adversity**
/ed'və sıti/

noun

a difficult or unpleasant situation.
"resilience in the face of adversity"
synonyms: misfortune, ill luck, bad luck, trouble, difficulty, hardship, distress, disaster, misadventure, suffering, affliction, sorrow, misery, heartbreak, heartache, wretchedness, tribulation, woe, pain, trauma, torment, torture, More

Translations, word origin and more definitions

Life's unpleasant. It's vile, cruel, and hateful. If we make it to be that way.

Every adverse environment brings with it the seed of advantage. Adversity is defined by Webster as "A difficult or unpleasant situation." I could say a few choice words, and many of you would find that adverse, right?

I could tell you a story about a little girl that was raped and then had her unborn baby killed inside her because her abusive Baptist preacher father decided to beat her nearly to death for going out drinking and getting raped, like it was it was her fault. Again, many people would find these words adverse, but how do you think my sister felt?

Or how about I tell you a story of a little boy that was never loved. Instead of hugs and kisses, he got beat in the head with a hammer or punched in the face. He was beaten and tormented for little things, but mostly because his father was a psychopath. I could go on and on, story after story, and again, you may find it adverse to just read those lines, but for me, those are the memories of my very unpleasant childhood. I lived through all those adverse situations, and after many years of useless self-pity and rage, I consciously chose to believe at my core that every adverse environment brings with it the seed of advantage.

What do I mean by that? Inside the problematic and unpleasant situation, the genius mind will be happy, as the genius mind understands that in adversity lies the genius' greatest weapon. The genius welcomes this adversity for in it, it sees an unfair advantage that empowers and propels the genius above all other. And I'm sure that you, a complete stranger, have genius capabilities.

What happens if you prepare for adversity? If you embrace it? If you expect it, but do not accept defeat? Sorry to be honest here. I don't want to tell you some emotional story to "connect" with you. I don't want to spend time thinking of slick, PR, generally-approved F*@$ing words to force some impression upon you.

I just want you to grow the F*@$ up. Your adverse situation is a joke to someone else. It's laughable, really. Go cry a river about all the bad things that have happened to you; go to a support group; chat it out. Then, come back and see if that has helped you or your business. If it has, do it some more. If it has not, look at all of the adversity, open your eyes, and see who it has made you and how strong you are. Here you are, look at you. Alive, a beautiful, conscious creation. All those things you've gone through, your perspective, how simple other things must seem to you. How much stronger you are than others—your willpower and what you can endure. You are a F*@$ing genius now because of that adversity. Don't you see? It's your biggest strength—the power you have over others.

I won't ask for your trust. I won't pretend to understand the things you've been through or the struggles that you've had. I would offer you a theory that suggests the one-way arrow of time in which events in the past are finite (unchangeable,) and events in the future conform to a collapsible probability function. You, and only you, have the power to shape and change your future. The past is over—there is no changing it. Some may debate this, but almost all knowledgeable people would argue that you cannot go back and change the past. However, you can use it to shape your future for the better should you decide to do that.

If you expect life is getting better, it's not. Right now, as you read these words, you are slowly dying. How's that for adverse? Expect adversity. It's not done with you. It's still there, coming for you every second of the day. You might, if you're lucky, get a small break, but it will just be a break, and then life is going to shit on you again. You husband will leave you; you will lose your job—and then what? Oh yeah, even if you achieve every goal you ever set, you still DIE.

Will you see that as an opportunity? Will you look for the seed of advantage hidden in what the simple mind would consider "some F*@$ed up shit?" The genius mind will. The genius mind will understand that a seemingly adverse situation is just the package in which we find our biggest advantages.

Are you looking for that edge? That extra power? That greatness? Well, dear unknown reader, it is right there in that adverse situation. So please, embrace it; allow it to empower you. Do not feel unlucky for the adverse situations you face, for those are the things that will make you stronger.

I do not mean to belittle you or make it seem like all the hardships you face are nothing or insignificant, but I would ask you to remember that right now, as you read this, children are starving, someone's loved one was just murdered, another has just lost their child, many homeless are sleeping outside in the cold, while others live in constant fear of abuse like I did my entire childhood.

I understand that all of these adverse situations affect us, but it is us who decides how we let them affect us. We do have the power to find advantage in every one of these adversities.

How can I say this? How do I know it? For me personally, this simple mindset shift has been worth millions of dollars. Here I sit writing to you from the comfort of my own office with over forty loved employees around me, at my own company now valued at over $50 million. I look back at five years ago before this mindset shift, and I was homeless and just released from jail for the stupid things I did because I let seventeen years of abuse and torture fill me with rage and hate. I could not see that all of the things I had gone there for were my biggest advantages. It was only after I had this mindset shift that I realized that these things had no power over me, but in fact, they gave me power. I was able to face life in a positive way. You will now do the same.

ABOUT JON VAUGHN

Jon Vaughn lived a very physically and abused life for the first seventeen years of his life. These adverse experiences had a major impact on his life. For a long time, Jon turned to a life of addiction and violence to try to cope with his troubled past.

Jon eventually had a mindset shift one day and decided to begin to look at all the pain and suffering he had been through in his life as an advantage he had over others.

Today Jon Vaughn is the Founder and CEO of the software development firm Tier5, now valued at over $50,000,000. Jon's company focuses on building software applications to help businesses scale by providing software solutions for the entire business process from lead generation, lead nurturing, follow-up, conversion optimization, and payment collection.

You can get all of Tier5's software free for 90 days from
community.tier5.us

Made in the USA
Monee, IL
15 April 2020

26006471R00125